Story Structure

The Key to Successful Fiction

Story Structure: The Key to Successful Fiction

First Edition

Copyright © 2013 William Bernhardt Writing Programs

Published by the Red Sneaker Press

An imprint of Babylon Books

The author wishes to thank Ralph Bernhardt for creating the computer-generated illustrations used in this book.

Story Structure
The Key to Successful Fiction

William Bernhardt

The Red Sneaker Writer Series

Other Books by William Bernhardt

Red Sneaker Writer Series

Story Structure: The Key to Successful Fiction
Creating Character: Bringing Your Story to Life
Perfect Plotting: Charting the Course
The Fundamentals of Fiction (DVD)

The Ben Kincaid Series

Primary Justice
Blind Justice
Deadly Justice
Perfect Justice
Cruel Justice
Naked Justice
Extreme Justice
Dark Justice
Silent Justice

Murder One
Criminal Intent
Hate Crime
Death Row
Capitol Murder
Capitol Threat
Capitol Conspiracy
Capitol Offense
Capitol Betrayal

Other Novels

The Code of Buddyhood
Paladins of the Abyss
Double Jeopardy
The Midnight Before Christmas
Final Round
Dark Eye

Strip Search
Nemesis: The Final Case of Eliot
Ness
The Idea Man
The Game Master
Shine

For Young Readers

Equal Justice: The Courage of Ada Lois Sipuel
Princess Alice and the Dreadful Dragon
The Black Sentry

Edited by William Bernhardt

Legal Briefs
Natural Suspect

Dedicated to all the Red Sneaker Writers:
You can't fail unless you quit.

Writing is structure.

William Goldman

TABLE OF CONTENTS

INTRODUCTION

Welcome to the world of the Red Sneaker Writers. If you're familiar with this outfit or you've read other Red Sneaker publications or attended Red Sneaker events, you can skip to Chapter One. If you're new, let me take a moment to explain.

I've been writing a long time, and I've been speaking at writing workshops and conferences almost as long. Every year I see the same tableau staring back at me from the audience: long rows of talented people, most of whom have attended many conferences, frustrated by the fact that they can't sell a book. And wondering why. Yes, the market is tough and agents are hard to find yadda yadda yadda whine whine. But for those aspiring writers who do the work and put it out there but still aren't publishing…there's usually a reason. Too often enormous potential is lost because writers don't understand the fundamentals of storytelling. Sometimes a little vigorous instruction is all that stands between an unpublished writer and a satisfying writing career.

I always did my best to help out at conferences, but the large auditorium/general information lecture is not terribly conducive to writing instruction. And sometimes what I heard other instructors saying at conferences I thought singularly unhelpful. Too often people seemed more interested in obfuscating writing than explaining it. Sometimes I felt speakers were determined to make writing as mysterious and incomprehensible as possible, either because that made the speaker sound like deeper and more literary, or because they didn't fully grasp the subject themselves. How could that help anyone get published?

After giving this problem some thought, I formulated the Red Sneaker Road to Writing. Why Red Sneakers? Because I love my red sneakers. Because they're practical, flexible, sturdy—and bursting with style and flair. In other words, exactly what I think writing instruction should be. Practical and flexible and useful, but still designed to unleash the creative spirit, to give the imagination a platform for creating wondrous work.

I started reaching out to other Red Sneaker writers with an annual conference. I invited the best teachers I knew, not only people who had published many books but people who knew how to share what they had learned over the years. Then I launched my small group seminars—five intensive days with a handful of aspiring writers. This gave me the opportunity to read, edit, and work one-on-one with individuals so I could target their needs and make sure they got whatever would help them most. This approach worked extremely well and I'm proud to say a substantial list of writers have graduated from my seminars and published work with major publishers. But not everyone is able to fly wherever I am to attend a seminar, and I couldn't justify traveling from home to work with one or two writers. What to do?

This book, and the other books in the Red Sneaker book series, are designed to address that problem. Short inexpensive books providing writers with the help they need. Let me see if I can anticipate your questions:

Why are these books so short? I've tried to expunge the unnecessary. I'm paring it down to the essential information, practical and useful tips that can improve your writing. Too many educational books are padded to fill word counts. That's not the Red Sneaker way.

Why so many different books instead of one big book? So people can find the information they need without losing a lot of writing time (though if you want to buy all the Red Sneaker books, knock yourself out). Each of these books can be read in a single afternoon. Take a day off from your writing schedule and read the book. Make notes in the margins. See if that doesn't trigger ideas for your own work. I bet it will. And then the next day, you can return to your writing schedule.

Why does each chapter end with exercises? Is this just padding? No. The exercises are a completely integrated and essential part of this book. Samuel Johnson was correct when he wrote: Scribendo disces scribere. Meaning: You learn to write by writing. I can gab on and on in my erudite and incredibly intelligent way, but you won't really learn any of this until you put it into practice. So don't get in such a hurry that you don't get the full benefit out of this book. Take the time to complete the assignments, not only because it may improve your next effort, but also because it will help concretize these ideas in you brain. I've also included a short summary at the end of each chapter, so you can review what you've learned at a later date.

I also send out a free monthly newsletter, filled with writing advice and market analysis and other items of interest to Red Sneaker Writers. If you'd like to be added to the mailing list, sign up at my website: www.williambernhardt.com. You may also be interested in my DVD set, *The Fundamentals of Fiction*, also available on my website. It's about five hours of me talking about writing. Who doesn't want that?

Okay, enough of this warm-up act. Read this book. Then write something wonderful.

William Bernhardt

CHAPTER 1: WHAT IS STRUCTURE?

And as imagination bodies forth the forms of things unknown, the poet's pen turns them to shapes, and gives to airy nothings a local habitation and a name.

William Shakespeare

Structure is one of the most important concepts for a writer to understand—and ironically, one of the least frequently taught. I have attended many writing conferences during my three decades as a professional writer, but the only time I've ever heard anyone lecturing on structure was when I was doing it myself.

Since story structure is so important, why isn't everyone talking about it? Is this structure business a dark secret that only William Bernhardt and a small cult of red-sneakered weirdoes understand? No (though that would be more fun). But many writers are reluctant to talk about structure, for understandable reasons. Books should be a realm that brings only insight and reward, but unfortunately, for some it has become a realm of snobbery and pretension. Consequently, writers become defensive. They fear that if they admit to any process or forethought in their writing, the hyenas will brand them as hacks. Outline? Oh, heavens no. What do you take me for, some penny-a-word drudge? Perish the thought. Artistes don't think about such mundane matters as structure and outlines.

Or do they? You might well be confused. At one time or another you've probably heard an author interviewed on television, or perhaps at a book festival. Do you recall any discussion of all the time they spend on structure? Or outlining? Or did you hear something like, "Oh dear me no. Each day I sit down in my quiet lonely writing garret with my quill pen, and I let my mind wander to a happy place of quiet creativity, and the muse rests on my shoulder and whispers in my ear, and the words bubble forth spontaneously…"

Please. Why would you believe anything a fiction writer says anyway? These are people who make stuff up for a living. (At this point, you may question whether the book currently in your hands is trustworthy, since it was written by…me. Fear not. I am the one fiction writer who never lies.) Here's the reality: Most professional writers engage in some form of preplanning. They may or may not call it outlining, but for all intents and purposes, that's what it is. It may not involve the use of Roman numerals or indented subheadings, but that's still what it is.

Author interviews can sometimes be fascinating for the insight they give into the origin of books or a writer's personality, but they are not reliable places to learn about the writing process. And that's unfortunate, because I don't think a writer can succeed without at least an intuitive understanding of the structure of stories.

You might well wonder why the concept of writing "from inspiration" sounds so romantic and literary. Writing "from inspiration" usually translates to "writing the first thing that pops into your head." While that might be more fun, it is less likely to lead to optimal results. I always tell my students to discard the first thing that pops into their heads. There's a reason why it came to you so quickly—it's not original. You've read it before, heard it before, or God forbid seen it on television. It's old hat. Cliché. Throw it out and come up with something better.

Which leads to another good reason to outline: to give yourself a chance to consider the big picture rather than making it up as you go along.

Bottom line: You need to get structure.

Happily, you've come to the right place. Here in the Red Sneaker universe, we strip away the pretense and abstractions that do more to complicate writing than to illuminate it. In the Red Sneaker School, we provide down-to-earth advice designed to improve the quality of your work. That will not make your work formulaic or crush your creative spirit. But it might help you produce better work so you can publish.

Isn't that what you want?

Writing Without Fear

Writers should not fear structure. Musicians don't. If you're a classical musician and you sit down to write, you will choose a musical form—binary, tertiary, rondo, whatever. No one criticized Beethoven because all his symphonies have four movements. For that matter, no one criticized Picasso because he knew how to mix paints to get the color he wanted. All art has structure, so there's no reason to shy away from it.

Here's the reality: Writing is hard. I don't say that to discourage you. Just the opposite. I say it so you won't become discouraged when your first masterpiece doesn't spring forth overnight and you don't get published the next day. Writing is as hard as anything you are ever likely to do. Story is complex. Characters can be elusive. Plot and presentation can be daunting. Style can be frustrating. So you should welcome any tools that aid you in this challenging but eminently worthwhile quest. And structure, once you understand it, is a tool that will make your work a thousandfold easier. Which is not to say it will ever be easy. But easier.

Writing a novel is a big project. The average novel comes in around 100,000 words, which amounts to about four hundred manuscript pages. The novelist must juggle numerous interrelated elements and somehow produce a synthesis that not only works but is also a pleasure to read. With such an immense project, it's easy to become overwhelmed. If you just sit down and start writing Page One without any preplanning or forethought about where this might be going, chances are the results will not be pretty. Sure, you may be able to revise and rewrite that first draft and eventually get it into shape (maybe) but wouldn't it be better if you produced a stronger starting place? Wouldn't it be better if the first draft, imperfect though it might be, already had the shape of a real novel? An understanding of structure should help you get from the blank page to the first word, and then the second word, and then the first chapter...and all the rest of the way through the book.

When I work with writers, I recommend that they take time to plan what they're writing before they write it, no matter how eager they are to start. Draw a diagram of your story (as you will see me do throughout this book). Organize your ideas. Outline. It takes some time, but ultimately it will make the process quicker, less painful, and more productive. It will help you write the book you want to write.

Highlights

1) An understanding of story structure is critical to writing a first-rate novel.

2) There is nothing wrong with planning your story before writing it. Most of the best novelists do.

3) Structure can help you grapple with the seeming immensity of a novel.

Red Sneaker Exercises

1) If you have not yet started writing your book, or even if you have, make a writing schedule. Treat that commitment as you would any other job. Show up on time and do what you promised to do. At the end of this book, in Appendix D, you will find a suggested Writing Schedule. See if you can make it your own.

2) Commit to writing a certain number of hours every single day. That's the best way to get a book finished. When you write every day, you'll find that your subconscious works on the book even when you aren't, which means ideas will spring up when you least expect them, making the times you are writing much more productive. If you're serious about being a writer, check out the Writers Contract attached as Appendix E—and sign it. But beware—if you sign it, it will be legally binding, because it was drafted by an actual attorney. Me.

3) In your writing schedule, allow yourself time to plan your novel before you write it. Read this book, make notes, prewrite, jot down ideas, and eventually write an outline (more on that later).

CHAPTER 2: STRATEGICALLY ARRANGING LIVES

The White Rabbit put on his spectacles. "Where should I begin, please, your majesty?" he asked.

"Begin at the beginning," the King said, very gravely, "and go on till you come to the end; then stop."

Lewis Carroll

Sometimes people have attended my presentations on structure thinking they are going to hear about plot. Plot is an entirely different matter, and as you may have guessed, also the subject of an entirely different book. Plot concerns the specific events you concoct to keep your characters moving on their journey. Structure is about design. When you create your plot, you are the construction worker building the building. When you think about structure, you are the architect.

Structure is the foundation upon which the story is built and the framework that holds it together. That framework of course contains many different elements, such as character, conflict, tension, and action. But structure is the glue that holds it all together. Of course writing involves many different elements, and the first-rate writer should master all of them. But if you've observed the fundamentals of structure, chances are your book will hold together. And if you have ignored the fundamentals of structure, or never knew them, the chances that you will stumble onto a satisfying story are seriously diminished.

All right, enough with the introduction. What is structure, anyway?

Structure is the selection of events from characters' lives strategically arranged to serve the writer's purpose.

Events From Characters' Lives

The first aspect of this black-letter definition concerns characters' lives. You may be wondering: Do characters have lives? I mean, sure, they live inside my head, but they are in fact fictional and thus do not actually have lives. Right?

Wrong. Very wrong. Your main characters should have lives and you should know those lives from start to finish, which is why I have students complete assignments such as writing job applications or resumes or Facebook pages for their main characters. You should know your primary characters' lives from cradle to grave. And once you have that thorough understanding of your characters, their backstory, where they are now, and where they are headed, it will be much easier to extract the moments from their lives that will advance the story you want to tell.

Before I wrote *Primary Justice*, the first of the Ben Kincaid books, I had a CHARACTER DETAIL SHEET I'd obtained at a conference somewhere. I took the time to fill it out for Ben and Christina and some of the other major characters, not so much because my brilliant

10

foresight told me this would be useful as because I didn't know how to start so I procrastinated. By the time I was done, I knew Ben's life from start to finish. Most of that never appeared in the book. But it did help me obtain a clearer view of who this person was so I could do a more consistent and convincing job of writing him. Little did I know that *Primary Justice* would be a huge hit and that over the years I would write seventeen more books starring that character. I could not possibly foresee that. But all that work I invested in understanding Ben's life paid off.

I was working on another book in those early days, at the time *Primary Justice* finally sold. This was my important serious literary novel, *The Code of Buddyhood*. For many months, I went back and forth between the two books. *Primary Justice* was a mystery/thriller, and *Code* was more arthouse fiction. Totally different, right? *Primary* focused on two old college buddies named Ben and Mike. Ben was the shy intellectual one, and Mike was more outgoing, charismatic, and street-smart. *Code* focused on two old college buddies named Bobby and Mark. Bobby was the shy intellectual one, and Mark was more outgoing, charismatic, and street-smart...

Are you detecting a pattern? Truth is, at the time I wrote these books, I had never published anything, and I had no reason to believe these books would fare any differently, so there was no reason not to borrow from myself. I created characters, got to know them, and then used them over and over again. You may think I lacked inspiration. I prefer to think of myself as creatively thrifty.

Here's my point: Ben and Bobby are the same person. Mike and Mark are the same person. I know their lives from start to finish, and they are the same lives, so much so that when *Code* was finally published, I wondered if I needed to change things around a bit. (My editor assured me that I did not.) But how can these characters inhabit the same lives when *Primary Justice* is so different from *The Code of Buddyhood?* The difference, my friends, is not in the lives, or the type of characters, or what they do with their lives. The difference is in the events I strategically selected to tell my story.

In both books, the characters went to school together, then drifted apart and entered their professional lives, then were reunited after a number of years. But in *Primary*, since it is a mystery, I focused on the events that led Ben to join a big law firm and get a case that drew him into the murder of an elderly gentleman and his adopted brain-damaged daughter. In *Code*, since it is a coming-of-age novel gravitating around these two men's friendship and how it changes over time (or doesn't when it should), I chose the scenes that focused on the friendship, how it developed, came apart, came back together again, and eventually became completely toxic. Two different stories. But the same two characters sharing the same lives.

Both books are still in print, so you can check this out for yourself. (In fact, you probably want several copies, so you can make lots of notes in the margins.) Why are the two books so different if they both have the same characters? It all has to do with structure. The books are different because I chose different events from their lives. Life is composed of millions of moments. Your job as a writer is to select the ones that best tell your story.

Strategic Arrangement

Some aspiring writers may get their dander up at the suggestion that they should do anything strategically, because once again, that sounds too much like planning ahead. I hope you can put those notions out of your head. A novelist must be a master strategist. A novelist must be the Napoleon of the keyboard. Each book has a thousand different elements that must be arranged, just as generals arrange their troops on the battlefield. Strategy is not a dirty word. Strategy means that you're a professional, someone who knows what they're doing. A team of trained monkeys can type the first words that come into their heads. A writer has a plan.

Strategic arrangement has two components: first, selecting the events from your characters' lives, and second, putting them in the proper order. In most cases, you will put them in chronological order, but that's not the only choice, and it's always worth considering other possibilities. *Catch-22* is not told in remotely chronological order, but the seeming randomness of the narrative reinforces the randomness of what happens in war. Similarly, *Slaughterhouse-Five* tells Billy Pilgrim's tale out of order (though it is anything but random), because he has come unstitched in time. Kurt Vonnegut deliberately uses this narrative technique to destroy the traditional notion of cause and effect and to show how powerless we are to control our own lives because the forces that surround us are so much more powerful than we are. Vonnegut is probably also illustrating the ludicrousness of any notion of "a cosmic master plan."

The film *Memento* made a fairly ordinary crime story fascinating by telling it in reverse order through the viewpoint of someone suffering from short-term memory loss. Harold Pinter's *Betrayal* tells a love story in reverse order, from breakup to first meet. In each case, the strategic choice and arrangement of events made the story unique

13

and helped the authors achieve their purposes. (The last chapter of this book discusses other nontraditional approaches to storytelling.)

The Writer's Purpose

At this point, you may be thinking that your primary purpose is to tell a good story. That's okay. Nothing wrong with that. We need more good storytellers. But your tale may be better told with some events than others. Much of my revision usually revolves around deciding what to leave in and what to take out. My first drafts are typically all-inclusive, everything I can think of that might possibly be good. In later drafts, I try to be more judicious. When it comes to leaving clues, for instance, the trick is to give the reader just enough information that the big surprise, when it arrives, will seem fair—without giving so much information that the reader sees it coming. Similarly, reader interest can be intensified by not answering all the questions right from the start. Let them wonder. Delay explanations. Mystery is good (though confusion is not).

As you will see in the subsequent chapters, the placement of the key events in your story can have a huge impact. That's why you plan. What does the reader need to know when? What character clues need to be planted so the reader will grasp the inner conflict without being told? How do I surprise without resorting to coincidence? How do I build toward a dramatic climax? These critical questions (and many others) will be discussed in subsequent chapters.

In addition to telling your story as best it can be told, the most resonant stories have a secondary purpose: to stir ideas and emotions in the reader. A book that tells a great story can be immensely enjoyable—and immediately forgotten. But a story that triggers new ideas, thoughts, beliefs, perceptions, or understandings is much more likely to linger. A book that moves readers on an emotional level, that makes them laugh or cry or feel inspired, is more likely to be remembered and chatted about at the workplace water cooler the following morning. And that is a good thing, because word-of-mouth advertising is the best advertising a writer ever can or ever will receive. Books that move readers emotionally are also those most likely to change human hearts and minds, to transform society, and to withstand the test of time.

Do an exercise with me, right now. Make a list of your three favorite books of all time. The books that mean the most to you. I know, you're already complaining because there are so many wonderful books you can't narrow it down to only three. Humor me. What are the three books that have meant the most to you over the years? Books you remembered long after you turned the final page. Books that made you laugh or cry or feel good to be alive. Books you keep on your desk beside the word processor because they inspire you so. Books that are tattered because you've reread them so many times. (Chances are, at least one of these books will be something you read when you were young. Don't be afraid of that.) No one is going to see your list, so you don't have to impress anyone. No need to list James Joyce's *Ulysses* or Proust's *In Search of Lost Time* (unless they really are your favorites). This is not a list of what you think might be the most important books of all time. This is a list of your *favorites*.

Now look at the list. Do the books have anything in common? Chances are they do. Chances are they have some common theme, purpose, or emotional resonance. If you can't see the connection, email the list to me and I'll tell

15

you what it is. And remember the connection when you're reading my book on Theme, because you responded to those books for a reason. They touched something deep inside you. If that theme touched you, it likely will touch others. This may be something you should write about. It may be something you're already writing about and just don't realize it.

Take another look at the list. Did each of these books produce a specific emotional response when you read it? Did it stir ideas or emotions? Chances are the answer is yes and that's why the book has lingered so in your memory. When a book makes you laugh or cry, when it gives you that glorious feeling of catharsis or epiphany, or a vicarious sense of adventure, you remember it. Who doesn't recall crying over *Jane Eyre* or *Wuthering Heights*? Or laughing over *Catch-22* or *Pride and Prejudice*? Or feeling inspired by *A Tale of Two Cities* or *Les Miserables*? There are many other media for the delivery of stories these days, all of them easier than reading—television, movies, audiobooks, etc. But nothing delivers the same punch as a well-written book. That's why we still read. And that's probably at least in part why you want to write.

Think about your book. What emotions do you want to stir? Nicholas Sparks has made a fortune spilling tears. Dickens was expert at it, too. Or perhaps you want to amuse, an approach that worked well for P.G. Wodehouse and Janet Evanovich. Perhaps you want to inspire your reader by creating characters who exemplify courage and self-sacrifice. All of these are worthy goals. But you need to choose the right events and you need to put those events in the right place to achieve your goal.

Instead of stirring emotions, or perhaps in addition, you may wish to stir ideas. Perhaps you see your book as delivering a potent message on an important subject, one readers will benefit from absorbing. This has been the ultimate purpose of many a great book. *Uncle Tom's Cabin*. *Little Dorrit*. Perhaps yours will be next. Often novels tell what is called an education story, or a coming-of-age story. Basically, the protagonist learns something valuable as a result of the events of the story...and ideally, the reader learns the lesson at the same time, without having to undergo the traumatic events the character experienced. This can make for a wonderful book, but it requires the writer to strike a delicate balance between subtlety and preachiness.

We loved Aesop's *Fables* when we were young, but the idea of telling a story that has a moral seems a bit obvious and old-fashioned for twenty-first century fiction. We benefitted from the New Testament parables, too, a different kind of story with readily perceivable morals. But the best novels are usually subtler, and for a good reason. Some people resist didactic preaching. Most messages are best delivered with just enough to allow the reader to get there themselves, rather than cramming it down their throats. When you announce the moral in big capital letters, it rarely makes much impact and often turns readers off. You've probably heard the famous quote from movie impresario Samuel Goldwyn: "If you want to send a message, call Western Union." Or a similar quote from Broadway's George S Kaufman: "Satire is what closes on Saturday night." As soon as readers detect that you're proselytizing, the entertainment quotient tends to diminish.

Of course, if you're too subtle, you take the risk that some readers will not get it. Believe me, it happens. Protect yourself by making sure your story is so strong that even if some lunkhead misses the larger meaning, they will still enjoy a riveting tale. Usually I think the best ideas are stirred by suggesting a possible answer, or perhaps merely raising the issue, then letting readers reach their own conclusions...in the context of the story you have given them. John Gardner suggested that theme was not so much about telling people what to think as announcing a topic for discussion and debate.

My book *Cruel Justice* is about being a father, or perhaps, about how hard it is to be a good father. That's the topic. I hope it stirs all kinds of ideas and emotions, especially if you are a parent or are thinking about becoming a parent. But I don't preach. I tell a story. I wrote this book shortly after my first child, Harry, was born, so you can imagine these thoughts were on my mind and of course they showed up in my work. The tale involves lawyer Ben Kincaid and a developmentally disabled youth who has been shuffled back and forth in the legal system until the boy's father, his only friend, gets Ben on the case. Ben is drawn to a local country club where he meets a struggling adoptive father who wants to be a good parent. He just doesn't know how. And we soon learn that Ben himself was seriously and dramatically estranged from his own father, though various clues suggest that Ben didn't know as much about the man as he thought. *Publishers Weekly* said this book was "Bernhardt's exploration of fathers good, fathers bad, and fathers never known." And this time, they got it right. I announced the topic, but no preaching occurred and no morals were shoved at the reader. There's nothing in the world more difficult than parenting. The point is to get people thinking about it.

Many years later I wrote a book titled *Capitol Conspiracy* (the sixteenth Ben Kincaid novel). This book took place after 9/11, after the Patriot Act and the subsequent public and secret infringements of traditional American civil rights. The book opens with a horrible terrorist attack and the death of the First Lady. Reactionary legislation is proposed to further crack down on terrorists—but at what cost? Ben and others must wrestle with the very definition of America, what it means, what it has meant, and what it will mean in the future.

Do we abandon the civil rights that are fundamental to America's identity in the name of increased security, or do we accept that freedom has risks and remain true to our original purpose? It's not an easy question and I don't suggest any easy answers. But the topic is addressed—implicitly—in a tale that primarily deals with trying to catch the terrorists and the inside operative running them. At the time I wrote it, just after we learned about the NSA's secret illegal eavesdropping on domestic phone calls (which no one seemed to much care about), it seemed relevant and worthy of discussion. But no morals were announced, nor was there any overt political agenda, though I'm sure some readers thought otherwise.

At conferences I have often heard it said that the purpose of nonfiction is to pass on facts and the purpose of fiction in to pass on emotions. This is completely wrong. Here's the truth: It's the purpose of both to do both. The best fiction will educate readers on a subject of interest that the writer has thoroughly researched. I could point to at least one example of that in each of my books and most of the books I read. And of course a novel needs strong emotional content. But so does nonfiction. This is the difference between a great biography or history and a typical high school text. A good nonfiction writer helps you understand that historical figures had hearts and souls and needs and desires, just like everyone else. Stirring emotion is the writer's primary job function, regardless of what you're writing.

Okay, now you understand the goal of this strategic arrangement of fictional lives. In the next chapter, we'll discuss how to structure your book to accomplish it.

STORY STRUCTURE

Highlights

1) Structure is the selection of events from characters' lives strategically arranged to serve the writer's purpose.

2) You should know the lives of your main characters from cradle to grave.

3) In addition to telling a good story, a writer's secondary goal is to stir ideas or emotions in the reader.

Red Sneaker Exercises

1) List your three favorite books of all time. What do they have in common? Do common themes emerge? Did they produce a specific emotional or intellectual response?

2) Write a job application for your protagonist and antagonist using the form attached as Appendix A. Take your time. Do you know as much about these critical characters as you should?

3) You may have heard the term "takeaway," meaning what the reader takes away with them after reading a book. What do readers get from your book? How are they rewarded for spending their time in your fictional world? Complete the following sentences:

When readers finish my book, I want them to feel

_____.

When readers finish my book, I want them to think
_____.

Now how are you going to arrange your story to make that happen?

CHAPTER 3: THE ACT

Find your own quiet center of life and write from that to the world.

Sarah Orne Jewett

The first step in structuring your story is to divide it into acts. The Act is the macro-structure of novels. Your acts will represent the progressive movement of your main character through the story. I cannot tell you how many acts you will have, because there is no limit to the length of books (ask George R. R. Martin). In Hollywood, screenplay writers adhere strictly to the three-act structure, but that is in part because movies have a limited running time. Books can have more acts, but three is the minimum. Each of the three acts has a different purpose following the classification established by Aristotle about 2400 years ago in the *Poetics*: beginning, middle, end. Act I tells the start, Act 2 tells the middle, and…well, surely you've guessed the rest. If you have more than three acts, that simply means you have a longer middle section.

The Multi-Act Structure

Okay, fine, three acts at least. What's going to go in all those acts? Harder to say, because there's no formula for writing a book, and if you thought you were going to get one in this book you should ask for your money back (sorry, no refunds). All books are different, but I can offer up some rules of thumb that are going to be true roughly 99.99% of the time.

In Act 1, you need to establish who your protagonist is, on the first page or darn close to it. You need to establish the viewpoint character(s), be it first or third person narration. (Please tell me you aren't writing second person. Ugh.) Few decisions have more impact on how a story is told than point of view. You also need to establish the antagonist(s), even if you choose to withhold their identities for the present. You have to establish the central conflict, and perhaps some ancillary conflicts (sometimes known as subplots). This doesn't mean there will be no surprises in the reader's future. It means they should understand, generally speaking, what this story is and where it is going. Otherwise, the reader will feel dislocated, and dislocated readers tend to put books down and reach for the remote. Exactly what you don't want.

In Act 2 you pull forward all the elements you initiated in Act 1, complicating them at every possible opportunity. In Act 2, your character's situation should get worse, not better. And in the final act, of course, you wrap it all up while simultaneously making your character's situation more dire and desperate and exciting, leading at last to the climax, which wraps up the primary conflict in a satisfying and final manner.

Most importantly, you must end each act with something critical happening to your protagonist.

An Act is a series of scenes and sequences culminating in a major turning point in the protagonist's life.

24

STORY STRUCTURE

Each act will end with a major turning point. That's what marks the transition from one act to the next. Mind you, every scene should have some kind of change that affects the chief character's situation in some way. The intensity of the scene will vary depending upon the magnitude of what occurs. Some scene changes are minor and some are moderate. But each act ends with something major. A complete game-changer. Something that takes the story to the next level. It's these escalating turning points that keep the story barreling forward, accelerating toward the climax. This gives the story a sense that it is getting larger, not smaller, intensifying, not dwindling.

The Turning Point

Turning points can take many forms. The most obvious would be a dramatic event that alters your character's situation, but sometimes even subtle events can have enormous consequences. Many literary novels have involved turning points that are essentially internal. They are nonetheless major. The turning point doesn't always have to be an exploding bomb. Sometimes it can be the bombshell delivered by your wife, or boyfriend, or the guy next door.

Writing is an art, not a science, so of course there will be variations, but generally speaking, the turning point that ends Act 1 will be something that ratchets the protagonist's journey up to a higher level, say, by making a firm commitment, or by making quitting an impossibility. After this turning point, there is no turning back. The turning point at the end of Act 2 is typically the "crisis," or the dark moment, the point when it seems most likely that the protagonist will fail. In Act 3, the protagonist will respond to the crisis by trying something new, or receiving unexpected aid, or making an important decision or sacrifice. When that climax occurs, the reader should be gripping the book tighter than ever before. You have carried your long-suffering protagonist through a series of trials and challenges, and now he has reached the end of the line. After this, there will be no second chances. He's on a roller coaster ride toward the final resolution—one way or the other.

The end of Act 2 often presents the protagonist with a decision to make—a choice. If this is going to remain a gripping story for the reader, make sure the choice is a real choice. In other words, make sure there is genuine doubt or uncertainty, perhaps a choice between the lesser of two evils, two choices replete with negative consequences. The protagonist should face the most powerful antagonism ever, and thus must make this decision in the final effort to obtain his goal or desire. Do not make this a choice between good or evil—because the reader knows how that will come out 99.99%. Luke is not going to choose the Dark Side, no matter how many times Daddy Darth suggests it. Instead, present the protagonist with more complex choices and let him make a decision that will show us who that character truly is, or better yet, how much that character has grown.

You may have wondered about the word "sequence" used in the black-letter definition. A sequence is simply a group of scenes that fit together. (Now you're wondering what a "scene" is. Later.) For instance, the murder trial sequence in several of the Ben Kincaid novels will be made up of many scenes, which may not be consecutive. The murder trial is a big deal, people have been waiting for it, so you don't want it to be over too quickly. That's a sequence.

Back to turning points. In my book *Perfect Justice*, Ben Kincaid is vacationing in Arkansas when he is approached about representing a member of a white supremacist militia group who has been charged with the murder of a young Vietnamese man. Ben is initially appalled at the thought of having anything to do with this hatemonger. As he learns more about the case, though, he realizes that no one else in this small town will take the case, and the court-appointed attorney is pathetic. In other words, if Ben doesn't represent him, this defendant will not receive a fair trial. Odious though the man is, Ben has always believed that everyone is entitled to competent representation of counsel and a fair trial. This creates a moral dilemma with which Ben must wrestle throughout Act 1.

When Ben commits to taking the case—that's the turning point. That's the end of Act 1. Now the story has ramped up to the next level. Act 2, the middle, concerns Ben's investigation, which culminates in a disastrous revelation and major setback that I won't spoil just in case you want to read this book. That's the end of Act 2. Act 3 ends when you close the book—and it culminates with a satisfying conclusion and a feeling that Ben has grown as a result of this experience.

Easy? No, but if you think it through in advance, using these major game-changing scenes, it will be easier.

Diagramming Your Book

I've always disliked the expression, "A picture is worth a thousand words." Bit of a slam at writers, isn't it? I can think of many situations in which a word was worth a thousand pictures. But let me see if an illustration or two can help illuminate these structural ideas.

Here's your book:

You may not think it looks much like your book, but it is. The far left end of the line is where the story starts, and the far right end is where the story ends. That's the main plot. There may be other stories as well. Subplots might span the length of the entire book, or they might start and end at various points while the main plot is in progress. They can also overlap. I'm going to draw in the subplots as overlapping arcs, but bear in mind that this is not the only way they can be done.

The upward swing of the arc represents the rising action—the mounting conflict. The flatness at the top represents the confrontation or climax, and the downward swing represents the aftermath, or falling action. In practice, your falling action should probably be shorter than your rising action, but I was trying to make this look pretty.

Now let's divide the story into acts. For purposes of discussion, I'll assume you're writing a three-act book.

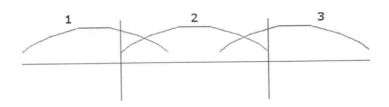

Those are the act dividers. You'll see I've taken the liberty of numbering them. You may also note that Act 2 is about twice the length of the other two. That's deliberate. The start and finish should be lean and fast-paced. Act 2 can be somewhat more expansive (though never boring). All those scenes I described that get the story started take place in that first quarter-section before the first vertical slash. All the breathtaking moments that lead to your climax go in the last quarter-section. And everything else fits in between.

We know each act needs to end with a major turning point, so let me draw those in now.

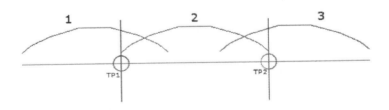

Those are your major moments, the crossing guards between one act and the next.

At this point, you may be wondering what goes on in all those blank spaces in the diagram. Fear not, we are going to fill up those spaces as you flesh out your plan for your book, filling them with excitement and character development and conflict. Lots of conflict.

Read on.

STORY STRUCTURE

Highlights

1) An Act is a series of scenes and sequences culminating in a major turning point in the protagonist's life.

2) The three-act structure is a good fundamental framework for storytelling—but you can have more acts in the middle, depending upon the projected length of your book.

3) Adding turning points in the key places gives your story a sense of acceleration so the reader feels propelled from one page to the next.

Red Sneaker Exercises

1) Start diagramming your book. Think about the main plot, then contemplate where the subplots fit in.

2) Identify the major turning points that end Act 1 and Act 2. If you haven't figured these out yet—now's the time.

3) Start thinking about your protagonist's journey. What will happen to this character on the journey represented by that straight line? How will you make your protagonist's situation worsen as the book progresses?

CHAPTER 4: THE INCITING INCIDENT

It has to start somewhere.

"Guerilla Radio," Rage Against the Machine

Readers can be infinitely patient with a book they enjoy and cruelly dismissive with a book they don't. One of my sisters once told me that she gives a book fifty pages, but if it hasn't grabbed her interest by then, she puts it down and starts something else. If true, then she is one of the most tolerant readers I know. Most will give a book about five pages, and some will give it even less. Of course, if the reader doesn't see something of interest when they picked the book up in the bookstore, they won't buy it in the first place. Perhaps this the result of the short attention spans of the so-called MTV generation—but I really don't think so. The truth is, we have almost endless entertainment possibilities these days, so there is simply no reason to stick with a book that is not providing intellectual or emotional pleasure. The television is only a click away, the theater is just down the street, and the Internet is always with us. For that matter, you can download a different book to your e-reader in mere seconds.

So you can see why it is of critical importance that you grab readers early on (and never let them go). This doesn't always mean that a gun has to fire on the first page. Sometimes more subtle approaches to seizing readers' attention are more effective, and certainly more memorable. In the Appendix B, you'll find a collection of some of my favorite openings. None of them involve torture, mutilation, the threat of imminent harm, or explicit sex. But all of them intrigue. All tickle the imagination. Some are funny, some sad, some grim. Here's what they all have in common: They are well-written, they are original, they suggest that you're jumping into a story that is already well underway, and they promise a great reading experience lies ahead. If you can come up with an opening line as great as these, that shopper at the bookstore who tumbles across your book will be far less likely to put it down.

It may be challenging to come up with that brilliant first page if you haven't figured out what's going to happen in the first chapter, or for that matter, how you're going to fill that first act. One of the most important, most fundamental decisions you have to make as a writer is deciding where the story begins, or more accurately, where your recounting of the story begins. Traditional wisdom says start at the beginning, but that might subject the reader to a lot of preliminary material that they don't need (at least not immediately), that won't seize their imagination right from the start. In school you may have heard an English professor discuss the concept of *in medias res*, a Latin term that basically means, "start in the middle." That's a good technique for drawing readers into a story. Start at an exciting point and save the exposition for later (or never). For that matter, while it may seem crazy to start at the end, some writers have done it. Harold Pinter's *Betrayal*, as I mentioned before. David Lean's *Lawrence of Arabia* for another.

So what's the answer, o writing guru? Where do I begin my story? The answer, probably not as helpful as you'd hoped, is to do what's right for your book. And you may have to experiment to figure out what that is. Many a time I've written first chapters I later realized were preliminary. They were relevant, but they didn't start the story. Which means they had to be cut, or perhaps relocated. Please don't start with chapters that flash back to the protagonist's childhood. Or provide a description of the weather. Or the landscape. Or throw infodumps and exposition at the reader. As quickly as possible, you need to introduce your main character and give the reader an idea what the world these characters inhabit is like—so you can turn that world upside-down in the inciting incident.

What's the inciting incident?

The inciting incident radically upsets the protagonist's life and instigates the journey to their ultimate goal or desire.

The Value of Chaos

The inciting incident is where the story really begins. There may have been preliminary events. There always are, right? But the inciting incident is where it begins in earnest for your lead character. In the book on Character, I discuss the importance of character arcs. For now, suffice to say that the arc, the journey, the quest, whatever it is, starts with the inciting incident.

This is the first major event of the story. The Big Hook. A major dramatic event. It can take many forms and shapes. But whatever it is, it is large, physically or emotionally. Subtle quiet inciting incidents do not produce highly engaging stories. Sometimes beginning writers, particularly those aspiring to write literary fiction, try to hide the ball, that is, try to underplay every event to such an extent that the impact on the protagonist becomes virtually invisible. I'm all for subtlety where appropriate, but it's no excuse for a boring story.

Usually the inciting incident does not occur on the first page (though I'm not saying it can't), because the reader needs to understand what the protagonist's life was like before so they can appreciate the titanic upheaval the inciting incident creates. The inciting incident should take a world that seems stable and throw it into chaos. The rest of the story will be about the protagonist's attempts to restore order. To restore balance. To set the world right again.

Let's take a look at the individual pieces of that black-letter definition. Note the phrase, "radically upsets." The inciting incident cannot be a minor speed bump. If you're not willing to raise the stakes, not willing to think large, why do you expect people to be interested in your book? Sometimes beginning writers think this means the inciting incident must involve some gruesome event, or at the very least, death. Maybe that will work. Depends upon your book. But sometimes the most dramatic events in people's lives don't involve explosions or bloodletting. Divorce, disease, loss of a loved one, incarceration, job loss—all are major traumas that produce upheavals in people's lives. In Appendix C, you'll find a list of the most traumatizing events, according to a major study, that is, the occurrences with the greatest potential for disrupting people's lives. You need to figure out the right inciting incident for your book, the one that will catapult your character on their journey and put them on an inevitable nonstop road to the climax.

STORY STRUCTURE

Here's the only requirement: The inciting incident must have an impact on the protagonist. It must radically upset the protagonist's life. Maybe others are affected as well. But if there's no direct impact on the protagonist, how can it start their journey? Too many times in my small-group seminars I've seen manuscripts that started with some major cataclysm…and then we cut to the protagonist, who knows nothing about it. Or has at best mild interest once they learn. Too often this leads to what I call "television episode writing," meaning the protagonist takes on a mission for someone else, but it means very little to the protagonist personally. (Like the doctor, lawyer, policeman, etc., who takes a different case and solves it week after week in old-school television series. It's just not possible for the protagonist to have a personal stake week after week, so the writers stop trying and content themselves with saintly do-gooders who repeatedly get involved in other people's business for no good reason. You can do better.)

Series characters have become popular in books, particularly though not exclusively in the world of mystery/thrillers, because publishers think of them as plot insurance. The thinking is that if a reader likes one of your books, they will look at the next—but not necessarily buy it. If they read the plot description and it doesn't grab them, they might decide to put it down and await your next effort. But if it involves a series character, they will think, "Well, this doesn't really intrigue me, but I've got to see what's going on with good ol' Ben and Christina." Plot insurance. Too often this leads to books that are essentially interchangeable, books in which the so-called protagonist is basically a host or caretaker solving other people's problems. And sometimes that gets published, but it's never going to be the basis for first-rate fiction.

I have written many Ben Kincaid novels, but I always strove to find a way to make each story important and personal to Ben Kincaid. He may be helping someone else, but he also has personal stakes. The inciting incident radically upsets his life (as well as others). The outcome of the trial, or the mystery, matters to Ben on more than an abstract or professional level. There is more at risk than just getting drilled by a baddie. His girl Friday Christina is on trial, or he's trying save a client incarcerated due to a trial he lost years ago, or his childhood nemesis is being held up to public scorn…or whatever. If the story is not fundamentally about your protagonist, it's not a novel anymore. It's an episode of a television series I don't want to watch.

So make sure your inciting incident has a direct impact on your protagonist, if not immediately, then soon thereafter and with dramatic results.

If you're writing genre fiction (and there's a term that's losing meaning each passing day), to some extent your choice of inciting incident may be predetermined by your form. If you're writing a mystery, there's a good chance your inciting incident will be someone's gruesome and horrible death (unless you're writing a cozy, in which case the inciting incident will be someone's tidy and tasteful death). If you're writing a romance, the inciting incident may well be the meeting of the star-crossed lovers. Not saying it must be. But there's a good chance. In *The Maltese Falcon,* the inciting incident is the murder of Spade's partner, Lew Archer. We never even met the guy, but we know this is a big deal because we see how it disturbs Spade. In Steve Berry's thriller, *The Alexandria Link*, Cotton

Malone receives an anonymous email telling him he has seventy-two hours to deliver what the sender wants, and "if I don't hear from you, you will be childless." In *Gone With the Wind*, the inciting incident is Scarlett's first meeting with Rhett—even though Rhett won't be seen again for a good many pages. In all of these cases, the inciting incident starts the main character on their journey that will ultimately lead to the climax.

The need for an inciting incident is not exclusive to genre fiction. Literary novelists use dramatic inciting incidents to kick off their novels, too. In Anne Tyler's *Ladder of Years*, it's a middle-aged woman's impulsive decision to get on a bus and escape an unsatisfying life. In *Saint Maybe*, it's a car crash killing two parents. In *Noah's Compass*, it's an unexpected burglary and injury. None of these involve bombs bursting in midair. But all of them caused major turmoil and introduced chaos and uncertainty in the lives of their protagonists.

Visualizing Your Novel

Remember that diagram we drew of your novel? Time to add the inciting incident:

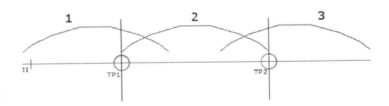

Note that I have not placed the inciting incident at the very beginning of the book. That doesn't mean you can't. You could put the inciting incident on the very first page. The inciting incident could even conceivably occur before the book begins. But if it does, the reader is likely to feel cheated (unless perhaps you flash back to it later, which I don't advise, but recognize as possible). If the inciting incident comes too early, you risk the reader not appreciating the import because you haven't established the protagonist's status quo prior to destroying it.

On the other hand, if the reader has not encountered the inciting incident in the first twenty pages or so, there's a good chance they're going to lose interest, even if they pretty much know what the inciting incident will be because they read the dust jacket before they bought the book. The average reader may not be thinking, "My goodness, where is that doggone inciting incident?" But until it occurs, until the protagonist's world is thrown into chaos and the protagonist has embarked on her quest, the reader is left with an unsettled feeling, a feeling of not knowing what this book is about or where it is going. So you need to get there as expeditiously as possible, but not so soon the reader can't appreciate its import, which is why I placed it on our diagram near the beginning, but not at the very beginning.

If you can't get to the inciting incident in the first twenty pages—what is going on during those first twenty pages? Should you fill those pages with character backstory, interior monologue, and directionless action? Definitely not. One possibility is to introduce one of those subplots you worked out in the last chapter. Let the subplot create tension for a short while until you've had a chance to set the major conflict into play. The subplot might be resolved somewhere in the middle of the book, but the main conflict will continue until the last word of the climax.

Those of you who have studied Newtonian physics (and what writer hasn't?) will be aware that for every action there is an equal and opposite reaction. Ergo, if you have a big dramatic inciting incident near the beginning of the book, logically, there should be another big incident near the end. In fact, since you want a book to have a sense of escalation, or of increasing size and intensity, there should be an even larger scene near the end of the book. And there will be.

The inciting incident leads directly and inevitably to the climax.

Highlights

1) The inciting incident radically upsets the protagonist's life and instigates the journey to the ultimate goal or desire.

2) The inciting incident must personally and directly impact the protagonist.

3) The inciting incident sets the fictional world into chaos. The rest of the book is about restoring order.

4) The inciting incident usually should occur in the first twenty pages.

Red Sneaker Exercises

1) What is your inciting incident? Why does it affect your protagonist so dramatically? Can you answer both questions in fifty words or fewer? (If you can, this can be the first half of your next agent pitch).

2) What subplot can you introduce to keep the story tense and interesting until the inciting incident occurs?

3) Remember your list of three favorite books? Can you identify the inciting incident in each of them?

CHAPTER 5: CLIMAXING

A writer is somebody for whom writing is more difficult than it is for other people.

Thomas Mann

A good novel is composed of progressive complications. To maintain reader interest, your protagonist's situation must get worse and worse. They can have the occasional small victory, so long as what's left unresolved is far more dire and important. Because the biggest sequence in the book must be the climax.

How do you make the climax big? Bigness can come in many forms. It may be a tremendous battle or fight scene (thriller). It may be a triumphant roll in the hay (romance). It may be an emotional epiphany, redemption, or the reconciliation of ancient wounds.

But it must be big. In fact, it must be bigger than anything that has gone before in your story. You don't want your climax to suffer by comparison to previous scenes, or to seem, literally, anticlimactic. Your reader has been waiting a long time for this, after all. You've been building toward it for three or four hundred pages (or a thousand, if you're Russian). Don't let the reader down. Give them a climax they will enjoy and remember.

Bear in mind that the climax will be the last part, or close to the last part, of the book your reader reads. A good climax will send them out singing your praises, recommending your book, blogging bout it, and giving it five-star reviews on Amazon. A lackluster climax will do exactly the opposite. Even if they enjoyed the journey, if the ending disappoints, they are unlikely to recommend your book. And in case you've forgotten, word-of-mouth advertising is the best kind a writer can get. So don't disappoint.

From Inciting Incident to Climax

The inciting incident leads directly and inevitably to the climax.

You saw this in the previous chapter, so perhaps now I should explain what it means. What starts in the inciting incident ends at the climax. Whether it is a quest, a mission, or a journey of enlightenment, the reader should feel it starting with the inciting incident and becoming fully and finally resolved at the climax. That straight line we use to visually illustrate your main story does more than mark the course of the book. It connects these two critical incidents.

I've heard some writing instructors call the climax the "obligatory scene," the idea being that once the inciting incident has occurred, the climax must follow. The protagonist may not initially understand that she is on a journey, or may not fully understand what the journey is. Nonetheless, that journey has begun and will not end until the climax. In the world-famous thriller, *The Da Vinci Code*, the protagonist, Robert Langdon, initially thinks he is looking for the Holy Grail. And he is, but as the book develops, it turns out the true grail is something far more interesting than a drinking cup. Nonetheless (no spoilers here, even though statistically speaking, most of you must have already read this book) the journey climaxes when Langdon discovers what the true grail really is.

Just to make this important relationship clear, I'm going to add another line to our diagram. I'm adding the climax.

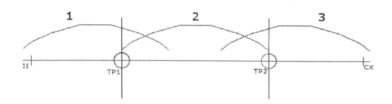

You'll note that, just as I did not put the inciting incident at the very start of the book, I similarly did not put the climax at the very end. We'll discuss what happens in those pages after the climax later in this chapter.

The Final Resolution

Now that we've established where the climax goes in this book you're writing and what its relationship is to the inciting incident, let's talk about what exactly the climax is.

The climax is a sequence that results in a final resolution to the protagonist's quest and a dramatic, permanent change.

Let me point out the key phrases in that definition: "permanent change" and "final resolution." (I assume you already realized the climax should be dramatic.) If your character is on a journey, and the journey results in a change, be it good or bad, positive or negative, enlightenment or disillusionment, wisdom or folly—the reader should feel the change is permanent. Otherwise, what's the point? No one wants to read about a journey to a change that only lasts a few minutes. The reader wants to feel this journey has been important, and you emphasize that importance by suggesting its enduring impact.

At the end of *Pride and Prejudice*, we want to believe that Elizabeth and Darcy have learned their lessons for good and will no longer give in to the titular temptations (which is why Jane Austen never wrote a sequel, though dozens of subsequent clueless writers did it for her). Moreover, we want to feel that this match is permanent and lasting and, to borrow a relevant phrase from children's literature, that the two will live happily ever after. That's what makes the book satisfying. The characters were on a long road strewn with many obstacles, but they overcame them and thus have earned their happiness. Most romances end with a union of the leads that seems permanent and lasting. We all know that, in real life, they may break up next week, especially since Elizabeth is rather strident and Darcy can be a self-indulgent prig (yet another reason why fiction is superior to real life). But for purposes of this book, the union is permanent and the two characters' quest for romantic happiness has been fulfilled.

Now that we've established the need for permanence, let's revisit the need for high drama, be it interior, exterior, or both. Your readers have been waiting for the climax a long time. They want a big satisfying payoff. Don't let them down. As I said before, if your climax pales by comparison to another scene, you've got problems. You might survive the problem. But your book will be better if the climax is the scene that leaves them gasping.

Let's consider another influential nineteenth-century romance: *Jane Eyre*. Here's where I risk incurring the ire of all the world's Eyreheads by suggesting that this book, brilliant though it is, is far from perfect. And its biggest flaw rests with the climax. This book, written during the great era of the triple-decker (books issued in three parts), is easily divided into three acts. The first act covers Jane's childhood, the horrible girl's school, and her eventual station as governess in Mr. Rochester's oddball household. The second act covers Jane and Mr. Rochester falling in love and the end of the act (the turning point) could not be more dramatic. Jane's wedding to Rochester is interrupted...(spoiler alert!) by Rochester's first wife, who is still alive and crazy as crackers. She's set fire to the attic, the smoke is everywhere, the madwoman is running around causing trouble, everyone is embarrassed, and Jane's moment of bliss is cancelled due to the troubling detail of her groom already being married.

Act 3 is tame by comparison. It has its moments. Jane runs off and ruminates on her situation, only to be lured back by some sort of psychic voice calling to her. She is reunited with her now blind but conveniently now single love interest. The story is concluded when she famously informs us that, "reader, I married him." Sweet, but from a dramatic standpoint, nowhere close to the drama and intensity found at the end of Act 2, which has left more than one reader (particularly the less romantically inclined ones) to feel the actual climax was something of a letdown.

James Cameron's accomplishments as a filmmaker literally go without saying. He's twice made the highest grossing film of all time, so I hope he will forgive me if I pick on one of his less successful efforts, *The Abyss*. This tale of underwater truckers has a fine cast, some exciting action—and one serious flaw, which is why it remains his least successful picture. The most dramatic scene in the film beyond question occurs in the middle. The female lead, Mary Elizabeth Mastrantonio, is trapped underwater with her ex, Ed Harris. They are both about to drown and there is only one scuba suit. In a bold heroic mood, Harris swims to safety carrying her on his back. By the time he reaches the headquarters, she appears to be dead. He tries defibrillation, CPR, mouth-to-mouth. She does not respond. He pumps her chest. Her eyes do not open. He keeps pounding and pounding, long after everyone else has given up. All the others in the room weep and suggest to Ed that it's time to quit.

At this point, the excruciating attempted resuscitation seems to have gone on forever....and then Mary flutters her eyelids and returns to the world of the living. This is one of the most painfully intense, nail-biting, riveting scenes ever put on film.

But there's one problem.

This dramatic high point comes in the middle of the story, not at the end. And nothing that happens later comes close to it in terms of narrative intensity. And there's some good stuff in Act 3. Harris is captured by aliens, they threaten to destroy the land-based population with tidal waves, peace is eventually brokered, the aliens' underwater ship rises to the surface, the two races meet. Interesting, to be sure.

But not nearly as dramatic as the near-drowning scene in the middle. Which leaves the viewer inevitably feeling dissatisfied—even if they can't put their disappointment into words. No one understood this better than Cameron himself. In an interview, when this film and its relative nonperformance were raised, he said, "There's a big problem with *The Abyss*. The climax comes in the middle of the second act."

I agree.

So, my writing friends, grasp the message here, just as James Cameron did. It's the same instruction you have perhaps received from other people in other contexts.

Don't climax too early.

Multi-book Epics

This climax presents considerable difficulty for people writing or planning multi-volume epics. Your biggest climax presumably should take place at the end. But that might be the end of the third book in the trilogy, or the fifth book in the tetralogy, or the last book in…whatever it is George R R Martin is writing. Each volume, each book along the way, must be satisfying in and of itself. That means each book should have a climax that is the biggest and most dramatic scene in that particular book. And the climax at the end of the final volume should be the biggest of them all.

Consider the Harry Potter series, the bestselling fantasy epic of this generation. The final blowout with Voldemort occurs at the end of the seventh volume. But each of the seven books has a climax of its own, the biggest most dramatic scene of that particular book, which seems to conclude the main action of that particular book (though of course Voldemort remains at large until the last hurrah). That's why each volume of the series is a satisfying read in and of itself, though each one also left you desperately awaiting the next entry in the series. That's the effect good, strategic planning and structurally well-executed writing has on a reader.

The Denouement

You may be thinking—wait a minute. The climax is the biggest sequence in the book, but it often is not literally the last scene of the book. You may recall that in our visual diagram of a book, the climax was inserted near the end, but not at the end. What comes between the end of the climax and the end of the book? Final Jeopardy answer: the denouement (some people call this the "resolution").

The denouement, a French word meaning "the unraveling of the knot," is literally that which occurs after the climax. You may wonder why anything needs to happen after the climax. Indeed, in many cases, the story will end with the end of the climax (the technical term for this is "open narrative"). In Hitchcock's films, there is rarely much denouement. Usually it is a matter of seconds tacked on after the climax of the final action scene, to assure us that that the bad guys have been dispatched and the couple on the lam will become lovers.

In my favorite, *The 39 Steps*, after the baddies are captured, we have a two-second scene showing the previously handcuffed lead couple grasping one another's hands. In other words, they like each other. Movie over. In *North by Northwest*, after the baddies are caught or tumble off Mount Rushmore, Cary Grant reaches down to save Eva Marie Saint...and the scene dissolves to him pulling her (dressed in sheer jammies) onto a bunk in a private Pullman car on a train. 'Nuff said—they're a couple now.

Hitchcock thought, probably correctly in the case of his movies, that once the action-adventure plot was resolved, the audience would lose interest, so he wrapped up the romantic subplot in an exceptionally expeditious fashion. Other writers are more leisurely with their denouements. J K Rowling famously added an epilogue after the climax of the final Harry Potter volume, flashing forward to show Harry in the future, married, happy, and sending his own son off to Hogwarts. This gave the books a nice feeling of cyclic action, of having come full circle. Was it necessary? No, and some people didn't like it for exactly that reason. But Rowling had learned to trust her instincts, so she gave her readers the assurance they craved that Harry, now Voldemort-free, would live happily ever after.

Most books benefit from some denouement, even if it's only a page or two to give the book a feeling of closure, to reinforce the main themes, to resolve character business, or to wrap up subplots. This is where you show that the protagonist and his world have changed. This is where you show the protagonist embarking on a new and better life as a result of the experiences of the book. What kind of denouement you write will depend upon what kind of ending you seek, what kind of feeling you wish the reader to have as they turn the final page. If you're after a happy ending, you show that, now that the main conflict is resolved, the central characters are happy (Harry Potter). If you're going for a more bittersweet ending, you may wish to show that, although the conflict has been resolved, the protagonist has paid an enormous price (*The Lord of the Rings*). Most television programs will end with some denouement, because it feels too abrupt to have the big action scene and then say, game over, turn off your tv set, go make a sandwich. So instead the cast gets together, recaps, jokes, and smiles for a few seconds. It reinforces the feeling that, although the inciting incident threw the world into chaos, the status quo has been reestablished. Almost every episode of *Star Trek*, regardless of where the Enterprise went, ends with the cast yakking it up on the bridge. And now you know why. This gives us the reassuring feeling that order has been restored and life, perhaps even a better life, will now commence.

STORY STRUCTURE

Highlights

1) The inciting incident leads directly and inevitably to the climax.

2) The climax is a sequence that results in a final resolution to the protagonist's quest and a dramatic, permanent change.

3) The climax should be the biggest and most dramatic scene in the book.

4) Don't climax too early.

5) Most books benefit from having some denouement, however brief, after the main conflict has been resolved in the climax.

Red Sneaker Exercises

1) Consider the relationship between your inciting incident and your climax. Can you fairly say that, once the inciting incident occurred, the climax was inevitable?

2) Is the climax the biggest scene in your book? If not, how can you make it bigger? Can you escalate the stakes? Can you put more in danger, or at risk, or perhaps make the risks more personal to the protagonist?

3) How can you increase the feeling of permanence, the feeling that the conflicts are now fully and finally resolved (even if you're secretly planning a sequel)?

4) Can you devise a denouement that will satisfy your readers? Are there character issues that can be addressed? Relationship issues? Something that will help reinforce your central theme?

CHAPTER 6: CONSIDERING EACH SCENE

You fail only if you stop writing.

Ray Bradbury

I wrote in Chapter 3 that the act was the macro-structure of the story. Similarly, the scene is the micro-structure. The scene is the atomic particle, the fundamental building block. Every time you write, you should be writing a scene. Since this is so elemental, you may well wonder why I didn't start here. Trust me. There is method to this incredible madness.

I have sometimes heard novels described as being composed of hills and valleys, or to be less metaphoric, scenes and sequels. The scene (or hill) is when something happens that moves the story forward. The sequel (or valley) is when nothing in particular happens, at least nothing that advances the story. It simply stitches the two scenes on either side of it together. In the traditional hardboiled detective novel, say something by Dashiell Hammett or Raymond Chandler, you will find scenes in which dramatic action occurs, shootouts and fistfights and macho confrontations. In the sequels, the private dick goes home to his shabby apartment, fries some eggs for dinner, pets the cat, drinks whiskey from the bottle, goes to sleep, wakes the next morning, feeds the cat, brushes his teeth with vodka, shaves with a dull razor, puts on the same suit, makes coffee with yesterday's used grounds, chats with the woman next door…and so forth. The sequel ends and the next scene begins when he continues working on the case.

I love some of those old novels, but at some point you might well wonder—if scenes are when stuff happens, why would we ever write a sequel? Good question. The modern style is to eliminate the sequels and focus on the parts that move the story forward. If you have some character business to establish or some mood to strike, fine. Do it in the context of a scene, an event, a meaningful exchange, rather than making the reader wade through pages of material that may strike them as essentially pointless because the narrative is not advanced. The amount of sequel you can indulge in may vary depending upon what you're writing. If you're writing a thriller, your reader will likely be little tolerant of any messing around. Story never takes a vacation! If you're writing women's fiction, or literary fiction, your readers may be somewhat more patient. But no one's patience is infinite. My recommendation is that you keep the sequel to a minimum and reveal character information, backstory, exposition and other non-narrative material in actual scenes.

In his terrific book, *Adventures in the Screen Trade*, William Goldman wrote that the best approach to a good scene is to leave out the beginning and the end (the parts readers can readily guess or that matter least) and jump from middle to middle. This makes a lot of sense to me. Too many starting writers give their books a leaden pace by writing a three-page setup for each scene before anything actually happens. Get on with it already. Start the scene when something interesting occurs. Leave out the rest, or describe in it one sentence, or just let the reader guess (if it doesn't matter). So you omit the introduction, the exposition, the excessive description, the musing aftermath—and focus on the conflict, the rising action, the complication, the clincher—and then move on.

Constructing Your Scene

A scene portrays an event that changes a character's situation in a meaningful way.

Some scenes are more meaningful than others, naturally. But the reader should always feel that the scene they're reading has a purpose. Otherwise the book will seem directionless and they will likely lose interest.

How do you make a scene affect a character in a meaningful way? Something important must change. This may mean your protagonist acquires a useful piece of information. Maybe they do something that advances them toward their ultimate goal. Maybe they suffer a huge setback. The change can be positive or negative, depending upon where you are in the story. What matters is that change occurs. This is what gives a story a sense of forward motion.

When you write the first draft of your outline (and just accept your fate already, you are going to outline), take a look at what you've got. If you see the suggestion of a scene in which nothing happens—delete it. Why would you include a scene in which nothing happens? Probably it's there to provide some backstory or other exposition, maybe to establish some character point or another. I must confess that in my early days, more than once I wrote a scene in which not much happens for exactly that reason.

57

Ben goes back to his boarding house, alone, feeds the cat, plays the piano, talks to the woman next door, eats some Cap'n Crunch, goes to sleep…is this sounding familiar? My point may have been to establish that Ben was lonely, to establish contrast with the more outgoing Christina, that he needed her. But all of that could have been more skillfully conveyed in the midst of a scene in which something of import happened, and in later books, that's what I did.

We Got the Beat

Some writing instructors, particularly those teaching screenplays, use the term "beat." The beat is an element even smaller than the scene, which I guess makes it the subatomic particle of stories. The quarks, if you will. Every scene should have many beats. What are they?

Beats are exchanges between two characters, typically actions and reactions, that combine to create the meaningful change of the scene.

Most scenes involve interaction between two or more characters. This can take the form of dialogue or action, which means the beats can comprise anything from talking to fighting to love making—or any useful combination thereof. One of the most difficult lessons for some writers is that dialogue can't just be two people chatting to no particular purpose (like so much real-life conversation). In one way or another—and some of those ways may be quite subtle—the dialogue must advance the story. This is most likely to be forgotten when the author's primary purpose for writing the conversation is to provide exposition—in other words, an infodump. Or where it's designed to reveal character. There is nothing wrong with revealing character, and some background information is always necessary. The

58

reveal though action, or advancing dialogue.

problem is that a scene that contains nothing but that will likely be static and slow and dull. Instead of letting the scene exist solely for these purposes, write a scene with many beats, many actions and reactions, that still communicates the information you want the reader to have.

Here's an example. Too often, I see starting writers dumping expository information much too early, like on the first page, before the reader has any sense of who the character is or any reason to care about their background. A better solution, assuming this background information must be revealed, would be to have it come out in dialogue. Better yet to have the dialogue exchange have an additional subtext that gives the scene tension, so there's something to keep readers engaged while they absorb raw data.

Imagine a scene between the protagonist and a lovely woman he recently met in the course of his adventure. The reader can feel the attraction. But he has a troubled past (don't they all?) and she's defensive because of a recently failed relationship, so the reader is uncertain whether they will connect. The protagonist starts to tell his story, but initially in a teasing sort of way. She teases back. (That's a beat.) He makes a sarcastic remark comparing his past to her past. She responds in kind. (That's a beat.) He becomes more aggressive, perhaps even challenging her to top this heroic tale from his past. "I took down twelve bad guys with one flame thrower." She one-ups him. "I took out a platoon with a bobby pin and a lipstick." (That's a beat.)

Finally he feels comfortable enough to ask her out. She declines, because she's been burned before, though there is a hint that she might change her mind when the adventure is over. (That's a beat.) Finally he suggests that, even though they have doubts about one another, since they seek the same goal, they should work together—but strictly on a professional basis. She agrees. (That's a beat.) Five beats have added up to a significant change—they're working together now, and much important character information about both characters has been revealed, without stopping the plot dead in its tracks. That's a win-win. That's good writing.

Scene and Sequence

A sequence is a series of related scenes that combine to create a passage of greater impact than the individual scenes.

The obvious example, which we already discussed, is the climax. Each scene may be terrific—finding the villain's lair, breaking in, cracking the computer password, fighting the virtual dragon, learning that the villain is really the hero's brother, being almost killed by his secret weapon, and finally vanquishing him with the power of true love. (Did you think I would waste good ideas on examples?) But together, all those individual scenes add up to one longer related sequence, and it's useful for you as a writer to see them as both individual scenes—what you might be able to write in a single sitting—and also as a composite sequence of great importance to your story.

Because Harper Lee originally wrote it as a collection of short stories, *To Kill a Mockingbird* is easy to break down into its composite sequences. We all remember the biggest one, the courtroom battle to save an innocent man, because it's longer and was featured most prominently in the film adaptation. But there are other sequences as well—Jem reading for the elderly neighbor, the kids going to church with Calpurnia, the kids being scared of Boo Radley, just to name a few. Because these sequences are Scout's coming-of-age stories, it should be no surprise that each of these sequences has a discernible lesson for her to learn. Fighting for the right is always admirable, though not always successful. The monster next door may be a sweetheart. The true monster may be the guy who looks like everyone else. Kindness can melt away meanness. And so forth. Each of these aggregated scenes comprises a separate but important sequence, and each contributes to Scout's overall education.

Producing Changes

You may find yourself struggling with the concept of producing so many changes in the main character's situation. Where are all these changes coming from?

Fortunately this question, unlike most about writing, is easy:

These changes in a character's life are achieved through conflict.

Conflict is the life's blood of story. What sound is to music, conflict is to story. Conflict should be present in every chapter, on every page. That's how you keep your readers turning the pages. This will be discussed in greater detail in the book on Plot. For now, suffice to say that you need conflict throughout the book. Different kinds of books will have different kinds of conflict, but fundamentally, there must be something that prevents your protagonist from getting what he wants, something that injects an obstacle or danger or risk to his quest. I have heard my friend Steve Berry say that "story never takes a vacation." What I interpret that to mean is that conflict never takes a vacation (at least not until the last sentence of the climax). Never take your protagonist's thumbs off the screws. Don't let the tension relax (at least not for long), until you're ready to release the reader and let the story end. Let your protagonist encounter repeated points of no return, seemingly impossible obstacles. Until finally all is resolved in the climax.

When you plan a scene, you should think about more than just what information you want the reader to get out of the chapter, or what needs to happen next in the plot. You must identify the source of the conflict. Conversations are more dramatic when they are steeped in conflict. Confrontational interviews. Cross-examinations. Fight scenes. Sex scenes. All better with conflict.

In each scene you write, make sure: 1) a noteworthy event takes place (in other words, something interesting happens), 2) as a result of that event, the character's life is changed in a meaningful way, and 3) the change is the product of conflict. Make that your writer's mantra: Event, change, conflict. Event, change, conflict…

Multiple Viewpoints

Since I repeatedly refer to the protagonist, some may be wondering how to write a book that has multiple viewpoints. That's no problem. First of all, even if you have multiple viewpoints, you have one protagonist. Usually. While it is not impossible to have more than one, this will not typically lead to the most satisfying reading experience. Readers prefer to be lodged in one character's head, at least most of the time. You can break away from that viewpoint on occasion, and that can be useful. In thrillers, writers typically cut to a different viewpoint to show what the protagonist's competitors or enemies are planning. The reader can see firsthand what the baddies are plotting. This allows the reader to know something the protagonist does not—which leads to suspense. When the reader knows about a lurking threat but the character doesn't, the reader has something to worry about. Something to fear.

You may also use multiple viewpoints to show trouble brewing. In the book *The Hunger Games*, the reader does not learn about the impact Katniss's actions are having in the outside world until after she survives the game and returns. That's because the book is written in first-person present, and Katniss has no way of knowing what's going on outside the game. In the film adaptation, though, immediately after the death of little Rue, the scene cuts to her home district so we can witness the rioting that erupts. This is not only dramatic, and a desirable brief change of scene, but also sets up the larger political story that will unfold in the future volumes.

Do multiple viewpoints impact our visualization of the book as a straight line? No, but it may add some parallel lines to the structure. Just remember that at some point, the lines must converge. The stories must intersect.

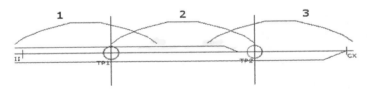

It's up to you to decide when those stories will intersect, but here's an example. The line above the center represents the story of someone competing with the protagonist to achieve the same goal. This might create conflict, but the character is not an actual antagonist. In my mind, the two will meet up somewhere in the middle of act two and start working together, so I've drawn the two lines converging in the middle of act two.

The line below the center, however, represents the antagonist (therefore, his line is darker). He will plot and scheme and cause trouble throughout, but he will not actually meet the protagonist until the climax, so that is where I've drawn the lines intersecting. The only requirement is that the lines must converge at some point, either at the climax or before. No matter how parallel the stories, at some point, it must all merge. This is when you give your reader the "aha" moment. Aha, the reader thinks, now I see how this all fits together. Very clever, this writer is…

Let me pause to answer a common question: How many viewpoints can I have? Well, that depends on your story, but for my money, if you can fully realize three viewpoints, you've done good work. Rarely do I think it's a good idea to introduce a viewpoint that will only appear in one chapter, i.e., a victim about to die. And regardless of how many viewpoints you have, it must be clear to your reader at all times that the protagonist is the most important character. If they are dislodged from the protagonist's viewpoint for too long, there is a good chance they will feel lost or disoriented and eventually will lose interest in the book.

Character Turning Points

Earlier I placed important plot turning points on our diagram at the end of each act. Even though this will be discussed in greater detail in the book on Character, I wanted to note that you should have important character turning points as well. Of course there's no rule on when they must occur, but I think it's a good idea to plan a big one in the middle of Act 2.

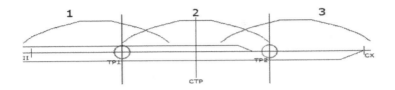

All too often, if a book loses steam, it's in the middle. Why? Often, when a writer starts the project, they have a clear idea of how it starts and a pretty good notion of how it ends. It's all that stuff in the middle that's a little fuzzy, and that fuzziness causes middle-of-the-book sag. Inventing enough increasingly challenging obstacles to fill the middle can be challenging. A character turning point (or two or three) can help.

So what happens in this character turning point? The main character is on a journey, remember, typically from one extreme or dichotomy to the opposite one. The character turning point may be when the reader first begins to see the change taking place.

The middle can also be livened up with some surprising plot twists. A plot twist is different from the plot turning points, or plot escalators, that I mentioned earlier. Turning points are those game-changing moments when the story jumps to a different place, a higher level. They may not be a surprise, but they are important. A plot twist, however, is by definition a surprise, and a good one. Something that opens your reader's eyes and makes then gasp. Makes them slap the side of their heads and mutter, Wow. Something that induces a smile, an appreciation of your ingenuity. And if you can plan a few good ones, you protect yourself against that middle of the book sag.

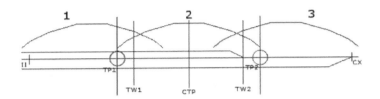

Finally, let's add in some smaller lines to represent all the individual scenes that will make up your book, all the changes along the way that will add up to a larger change at the end.

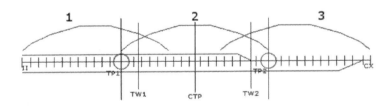

There you have it. A diagram of a complete novel. Can you construct a diagram for your story? And most importantly, can you identify all the key scenes and where they fall in the diagram?

STORY STRUCTURE

Highlights

1) A scene portrays an event that changes a character's situation in a meaningful way.

2) These changes in a character's life are achieved through conflict.

3) In every scene there must be: an event, leading to change, produced by conflict.

4) Beats are exchanges between two characters, typically actions and reactions, that create the meaningful change of the scene.

5) A sequence is a series of related scenes that combine to form a passage of greater impact than the individual scenes.

6) Multiple viewpoints can increase the suspense.

Red Sneaker Exercises

1) Think about the scenes in your book. Does each portray an important event in the life of your characters? Is each scene replete with conflict?

2) How many viewpoints will you have in your book? Why? For each viewpoint you're considering in addition to the protagonist, write a one-page justification or explanation of why that viewpoint is necessary and will improve your story.

3) Can you pinpoint a place in your story when your main character begins to change?

CHAPTER 7: PUTTING IT TOGETHER

When forced to work within a strict framework the imagination is taxed to its utmost—and will produce its richest ideas. Given total freedom the work is likely to sprawl.

T S Eliot

Are you beginning to see how these different structural elements work together? I want to emphasize that this structure idea is not something I made up, nor is it some modern academic invention. This is the structure of stories and always has been. You can take it all the way back to *Gilgamesh*, humanity's oldest surviving story (unless you count the tales arguably illustrated by the Lascaux cave paintings) and you will find it. You'll find it in *Beowulf* and *The Iliad* and *The Odyssey* and *The Aeneid*. And you'll find it in Lee Child and Jayne Anne Krantz and Orson Scott Card. This is the structure of stories. If you understand this and how it works, you can't help but be a better writer.

Let's see if we can apply this structure to some familiar stories. Just to be fair, I'll use one British book and one American, one so-called women's book and one for guys. *Pride and Prejudice* and *The Adventures of Huckleberry Finn*. Both great novels, both very different—but both still clearly employing the fundamental structure of storytelling, which is one reason the books work so well.

You probably know the story of *Pride and Prejudice*. Elizabeth Bennet and her many sisters need husbands, and the sooner the better. Her father is not wealthy and when he dies his estate will go to the odious Mr. Collins, leaving the girls potentially penniless in a world where women had precious few opportunities to generate income. So ask yourself—what's the inciting incident?

Answer: a new eligible bachelor has come to town, and Mrs. Bennet is all over him. Sometimes we make fun of Mrs. Bennet's single-minded obsession, but like any good mother, she's just trying to look after her girls, right? So when Mr. Bingley, a single man with a decent income arrives, she starts after him. Various complications ensue, some comic, some pathetic. What's Plot Point 1, signifying the transition from Act 1 to Act 2?

Answer: Bingley's ball. Why? Because that's when Elizabeth meets Darcy. This was supposed to be a chance for Bingley to meet the inhabitants of this country town, and for the females to pursue him. Elizabeth's older sister Jane does strike it up with Bingley, but Elizabeth's attention is occupied by the rude, surly, snobbish—but exceptionally wealthy—Mr. Darcy. Goodness knows why she's attracted, because he behaves deplorably. But it's easy to see that there's something going on between these two, right from the start.

Act 2 recounts one misadventure after another. The course of true love ne'er did run smooth, after all. Especially not in romance novels. Each scene has event, change, conflict, and as a result, the couple does not grow closer together. Elizabeth has embarrassing incidents and her pride and prejudice prevent her from admitting she is interested in Darcy. Darcy comes off as a complete creep and his pride and prejudice toward these gauche country bumpkins prevent him from establishing anything romantic with Elizabeth.

Until the Character Turning Point. Darcy sends a letter of proposal to Elizabeth. What? Where did that come from? This is a character turning point because it shows that, despite outward appearances, Darcy likes Elizabeth very much. Furthermore, even though Elizabeth rejects the proposal, one is left feeling that she objects to the proposal itself more than the concept being proposed. Darcy gives probably the worst proposal of all time, noting the faults in her family's behavior and how beneath his station they all are, and yet he explains, even though this will be a horrible match for him, he finds himself compelled to make the offer anyway.

Who could resist a proposal like that? Well, Elizabeth, for starters. This is the middle of the book, so we don't want our climax here. We want escalating complications, more conflict. But we can definitely see that attitudes are changing.

Plot Point 2, bridging Act 2 and entering Act 3: Something horrible happens, something so bad it shakes the Bennet family to its core. Elizabeth's youngest sister, Lydia, runs off with a soldier of ill repute. There is no way to diminish this catastrophe. Lydia's imprudent act has not only soiled her own reputation. If the public finds out—she has soiled the whole family, which means none of those sisters will ever find a husband. This is the dark moment.

In the exciting climax sequence, Darcy saves the day, locating the lovers and paying the soldier off so he will marry Lydia and make an honest woman of her before word leaks. The family honor is saved. At this point, Elizabeth can't help but acknowledge that, even if he is a little rough around the edges, Darcy's a pretty good guy. Which sets the stage for another proposal, this time accepted.

See how the elements fit together? *Pride and Prejudice* supplies all the structural elements of classical storytelling that I have outlined. Did this make it formulaic? No. Did this make it a trashy genre novel? No, this made it one of the most popular novels ever written. The book was improved, not diminished, because this extremely talented and well-read author understood how stories work.

Not let's consider *The Adventures of Huckleberry Finn*. What's the inciting incident? What's the dramatic event that throws Huck's life into chaos?

Huck's father, known as Pap, has disappeared. (We later learn he's dead, but Huck doesn't know because Jim doesn't tell him.) Pap was a loser, a drunk, a reprobate, usually unemployed—but he was the only parent Huck had. Now the boy has nothing. So he's adopted by the Widder Douglas, which brings him into the mainstream life of Hannibal, Missouri. The Widder is a religious woman who tries to civilize this wild child, without much success. Various hijinks ensue. But the book really kicks into high gear at Plot Point 1.

Huck helps Jim, an escaped slave. This is a big deal. Today, we see this sympathetically, but in Huck's time, especially in the South, it was a different matter. Thanks to the *Dred Scot* decision, slaves were considered property. Helping slaves escape was tantamount to helping a thief steal property. It was a crime. Worse, in the Widder's mind, it was a sin. A crime against God. Huck does it, without much thought at first, just going along with the ride. But that changes as the boy spends more time with Jim. In a great scene, he looks into Jim's eyes and sees the person inside, a person no different fundamentally from himself. Why is it okay for Huck to escape whenever he pleases, but not Jim? Why is Huck a free man and Jim property? In this classic character turning point, Huck begins to see that Jim is a person like himself, and in some rudimentary way understands what a horror, a crime against nature, slavery truly is.

Huck receives a letter from the Widder. She wants him to come home. She knows what he's been up to. And if he persists, she says, he not only might end up in jail—he's going to Hell. What's this poor uneducated boy to do? Everyone tells him he should turn Jim in. But he has looked into the man's eyes, and as a result, something in this kid's head instinctively tells him that slavery is wrong. Turning him in would be wrong.

So what happens? Huck rips up the letter and says, "All right then. I'll go to hell." Better that than be a part of this unjust institution. How's that for a character turning point?

Act 2 has more incidents, some dramatic, most played for laughs. But things turn dark leading into Act 3 (at Turning Point Two) when Jim is recaptured. Tom Sawyer shows up again, adding what some feel is an unwelcome note of comedy in this dark moment. But I think Twain knew what he was doing. He could address a dire situation without being completely glum. When the climax is resolved, Huck has committed himself to his instinctive understanding of right and wrong and helps Jim escape. Again. Huck heads off in his own direction, uncertain of the future and with many questions still unanswered. But there's no doubt but that he has been changed—

dramatically and permanently—by this experience. And despite his lack of formal education, he has proven himself a good deal smarter than most of the people around him.

By observing all the structural elements of classical storytelling, Twain creates a funny and moving tale that not only entertains but also addresses many serious subjects. Some have said that Huck Finn is the greatest American novel because Huck's conflicts, both external and internal, mirror the conflicts of America as a nation as we dealt with the evil of slavery.

Now let's see what you can put together.

STORY STRUCTURE

Red Sneaker Exercises

See if you can answer the following questions about your book. When you can, you're ready to proceed to the next chapter and outline. Some of your answers may be somewhat sketchy. That's okay. You'll flesh this out more when you actually write the book. What's most important at this point is that you have a grasp of the overall structure of your story. You will be amazed at how much this will help you when you actually begin to write.

1) What is the Inciting Incident? Does it take too long to get to it? What crisis does it create?

2) How does the Inciting Incident directly relate to the Climax?

3) What problem does the Inciting Incident create for the protagonist?

4) What problem does the Inciting Incident create for the antagonist?

5) What obstacles or points-of-no-return will the protagonist face? What is the worst possible thing that could happen to your character? How many times does it happen? How do the challenges test him/her?

6) What subplots sustain or complement the main conflict?

7) What major plot point signals the end of each act?

8) What causes the reader to become increasingly engaged in the story and fascinated by the characters?

9) What causes the reader to care more about or identify more with the protagonist?

10) Will the readers feel the acceleration of the plot in the final act?

11) What is the climactic sequence? Is it big or important enough to justify the journey to get to it?

12) What idea does the story ultimately suggest to its readers? What emotional impact will this story have on readers?

CHAPTER 8: OUTLINING

Writing comes more easily if you have something to say.

Sholem Asch

I'm not sure if people resist outlining because they think it will make their work formulaic, because they fear it will stifle their innate creativity—or because it sounds like a lot of work. Boring work. Much more fun to just start being creative and plunge in.

This plunge is what most writers would call a suicide jump.

Yes, outlining is work. It might well be more fun to just start writing the chapter you already have in your head. But you will benefit immensely if you put Chapter 1 on hold for a day or three and make yourself produce an outline. You may not appreciate what a difference it will make at the time. But you will later. I guarantee it.

Two points first. One: If your aversion to outlining comes from some suppressed memory of freshman English where the teacher made you turn in an outline for a grade, using Roman numerals and indented lines and all that—get over it. You're making this outline for yourself, so it doesn't matter what format you use. It does matter that you do it.

Two: Always remember that the outline is simply that. A guideline. A helper. It is not a cage. When you actually write the book, you will almost certainly get new and different, usually better, ideas. The further you go in the book, the more you will likely digress from the outline. Does that mean outlining was a waste of time? Definitely not. You might never have gotten to this advanced place in your thinking about the book if you didn't have the outline to build from. You can and will make changes as you write. That's as it should be. But because you have taken time to outline, you will never on any morning sit down in front of your word processor and have no idea what to write next. You will never gaze out the window and think, I don't know where this train wreck is going. Because your outline is right there to remind you where you're going, what the endgame is. No matter how many changes you make to it later, you will do better work—and probably work more quickly—if you take the time to outline.

Starting your Outline

This is not going to be as unpleasant as you might think. I'm going to walk you through it step-by-step.

Step 1: Go buy some index cards.

Is it possible to do this without index cards? Sure. But there's nothing easier. Yes, I know there are computer programs that will create virtual index cards, even a virtual bulletin board to pin them upon. And I'm sure there are some legitimate reasons for doing so, even if I can't imagine what they would be when you can get a pack of index cards at Wal-Mart for about seventy-nine cents. But whatever.

Index cards are portable, brief, and easily rearranged. You can lay them out on your coffee table. You can pin them to a bulletin board. You can tuck them into your pocket. You can reorder them readily.

How many will you need? That depends upon the length of your book, and only you can guess at that. But generally speaking, a novel on average has about sixty distinct major scenes.

Step 2: Count out sixty index cards. Arrange them in three piles—two piles of fifteen, and one pile of thirty.

Bet you've already guessed why. You're going to divide the cards into your three acts, then describe a scene on each card. You're going to put fifteen scene/cards in Acts 1 and 3 and twice as many, thirty, in the longer Act 2. Remember: All these numbers are approximations at best. If it turns out you need a few cards more or less for each act, don't sweat it. And if you've decided your epic will have more than three acts, that just means you need to count our more cards for that extra-long middle.

Step 3: Briefly describe the event that will occur in each scene.

Okay, this is going to take a little longer. My non-mandatory suggestion is that you start with Act 1. Most writers have a pretty good idea how they want their book to start (even if they change their minds repeatedly later), so lead with your strength. Do you know what your inciting incident is? Chances are you do by now. So write that card first. Do you know what the first major plot point is, that which divides act one from act two? If so, write that card next. Isn't this easy? Now you just have thirteen more cards to fill and you're done with this act.

What needs to happen first so that readers can fully appreciate the inciting incident and why it has such a devastating impact on the protagonist? Do you need to establish the character's normal routine, relationships, or world? Whatever needs to happen, write those cards next, filling the space between the beginning and the inciting incident. Are there any subplots you need to introduce here, to interject tension and keep the story from seeming dull before the inciting incident occurs? If so, write those cards. Are there any supporting characters, sidekicks, best friends, or significant others who need to introduced at this time? If so, fill out those cards. After the inciting incident, you will need to establish the central conflict, at least in its nascent form. Write those cards. Usually all viewpoint characters will be introduced in the first act. Write the cards. And finally, consider what events need to occur to get the reader from the inciting incident to the first major plot point. Write them down. If you've done all that, there's a good chance you've already filled out all fifteen cards. Good work!

Subplots can be an extremely useful tool for a writer. First, they give you the ability to inject tension into the book even before the main conflict has been realized. The best subplots will bear a plot-based or thematic relationship to the main plot. Usually this occurs because the thematic message of the subplot is precisely the opposite of that of the main plot—generating irony—or the thematic message of the subplot reinforces the message of the main plot, enriching the theme or perhaps showing its depth or truth or infinite variation. The subplot can also complicate the main plot. Many a love story has been interjected into a mystery or thriller because it makes the hero's work that much harder (particularly when the lover is taken hostage in Turning Point 2). In John Mortimer's clever *Rumpole* stories, the barrister Rumpole always handles a court case, but the theme emerging from the case is usually reinforced by a subplot involving his personal life or that of one of the other members of his chambers. Many readers probably miss this altogether, but for those who don't, it makes the stories even more enjoyable.

Here's a quick checklist of all the questions you must make sure you've answered for the reader in the first act:

Who is the lead character?

What does the protagonist desire? What is his/her goal?

What's the main problem? (perhaps ignited by the inciting incident)

What kind of story is this? (mystery, romance, thriller, coming-of-age)

What's the protagonist's plan for overcoming the problem? (Granted, the protagonist may only have a glimmer of this in the early pages, but they should at least have a glimmer.)

Who's the opponent/antagonist? (Again, the reader should at least have hints.)

Have you filled out all the cards for Act 1? Good.

You probably think I'm going to suggest that you proceed now in an orderly fashion to Act 2. How little you know me.

Skip ahead to Act 3. Why? Because even in the early stages, most writers have some idea where the story will start and how it will end. (It's the middle that most often remains vague.) So go ahead and write what you know. What is Turning Point 2, the big game-changing event that marks the transition out of Act 2 and into Act 3, starting the nonstop roller-coaster ride straight to the climax? Whatever it is, write that card.

Bet you've already guessed the next part. Write the cards that make up the climax. Note that I said *cards*. As we've discussed, the climax should be a big deal, so it will likely consume more than one scene, perhaps even cutting back and forth between different scenes and events to heighten the drama. Write out those cards next, and don't be stingy, baby. Play it up to the max. Make it as horrible and desperate and seemingly hopeless as you possibly can.

Do you have a denouement? Will anything occur after the climax? Chances are you will need at least a scene or two to end your story on the proper note. Write those cards now.

Here's my checklist of things that should happen in Act 3. Some of these may be more implicit than explicit, but the reader should get them just the same:

The moment of self-revelation, when the protagonist and the reader realize the character has changed.

The final confrontation.

The resolution of the conflict.

The beginning of a new life.

The resolution of character-related subplots.

At this point, it's simply a matter of connecting the dots, drawing the reader from Plot Point 2 to the climax. Write out those scenes, remembering that story never takes a vacation, so don't let the tension drop, don't let the pace sag, not even for a moment.

Filled out all the cards for Act 3? Excellent. And that leaves Act 2. For most writers, this will be where you spend the most time, because this is the part you have least worked out in your mind. No problem. That's why we outline. Don't get discouraged if this part requires more time and head-thunking.

STORY STRUCTURE

Write in your Character Turning Point and plunk it down right in the middle. Now you have a signpost. You just need fourteen scenes before it and fourteen after. Easy street.

Start by pulling forward all the threads you initiated in Act 1. If you started a subplot or subplots, write the scenes needed to advance them. Characters introduced in Act 1 should continue to have scenes in Act 2. Whatever it is your protagonist started out in pursuit of in Act 1, that quest should continue in Act 2. And regardless of what the conflict might be, remember that it must get more complicated, not less, throughout the second act. What was grim before must become absolutely bleak. What was difficult before must become all but impossible. If you haven't introduced your main antagonist yet, now's the time. All your main characters, in most circumstances, should be introduced before you reach the midpoint of the book.

For the second half of Act 2? You do the same, only more so. Pull all the plot threads forward. Make sure all your main characters have something to do. Make sure the characters continue to advance in their quests. Make sure the central problem becomes worse.

Here, you're probably hoping for another of my splendid checklists. That would be tough to do, since middles are capable of infinite variation. But here's one question to answer when you're outlining this act: Have I planted everything that needs to be planted to make the Climax and Denouement pay off the way I want it to pay off?

To "set something up" means to give the reader essential foreknowledge. That information may not seem important at the time (and you probably want it that way), but it will be important later. To pay it off means to create a subsequent scene in which that knowledge becomes important. You may have heard Anton Chekov's famous imperative: If in the first act you have hung a pistol on the wall, then in the following one it should be fired. Otherwise don't put it there." The setup is the difference between an ending that seems coincidental or contrived and a scene that works wonderfully well. This will be discussed in the book on Plot in more detail, but for purposes of outlining, make sure you've thought about how these critical pieces of information will be provided to the reader so your climax works.

Done yet? Filled out all sixty cards? Excellent.

Step 4: Put the cards in order.

Now that you have something written on all sixty cards, you may realize that the deck needs to be reshuffled. Maybe scene seven needs to occur before scene six. Maybe you have too many consecutive talking scenes, or too many fighting scenes. Break them up to improve the pacing and variety. Make sure the basic story and character motivations make sense.

Step 5: Type it up

You could just leave this in index card form, but for the sake of convenience and security, type it up. You don't need a fancy format. Just type (1) followed by whatever happens in the first scene, then (2), and so forth. You don't have to write in that much detail. If you already know what will happen in a given scene, by all means, get it down. But at this stage, "Ben calls the coroner to the stand" or "Christina interviews the accountant" is enough. Type it up, and then you have a document, probably under five pages, that is the outline of your book. You can take it anywhere. You can leave it on the desktop of your computer.

And now you are ready to write the book. Don't put it off. Start tomorrow.

Highlights

1) Go buy some index cards.

2) Count out sixty index cards. Arrange them in three piles—two piles of fifteen, and one pile of thirty.

3) Briefly describe the event that will occur in each scene.

4) Put the cards in order.

5) Type it up.

Red Sneaker Exercises

1) Draw a diagram like the one at the end of chapter seven and identify all the different elements of your story. Use this to visualize the progress of your book.

CHAPTER 9: CLASSICAL STORYTELLING

The art of writing is the art of discovering what you believe.

Gustave Flaubert

The structure I've described in the previous chapters is what is traditionally described as classical storytelling. Is it the only way to write a story? No. Is it the best way? Usually. Depends on what you're trying to accomplish. In the twentieth century, we saw much experimentation with traditional forms. But in most cases, for traditional books, and especially for beginning writers, the classic storytelling mode is the best. This is the form that has worked consistently with precious little change for the last four thousand years. It has probably worked since the first caveman with an imagination sat around the campfire and entertained his clan with a story.

Is it possible to tamper with these time-tried approaches? Of course. Writing is, at the end of the day, an art, not a science, but as in science, experimentation can sometimes produce interesting results. The era we now call Modernism produced many interesting exercises in literary experimentation as writers tried to break free of the old templates and create something more profound. For example, many writers experimented with stream of consciousness as an alternative to traditional viewpoint. The Postmodern experimentation was arguably even more innovative. It's worth noticing, however, that at the end of the day, most novels are still written in accordance with the fundamental principles I'm calling classical storytelling. Stream of consciousness was interesting, but ultimately resulted in only two novels I would call successful (*To the Lighthouse* and *The Sound and the Fury*) and Faulkner himself considered *The Sound and the Fury* a failure.

Yes, the Modern Library has said that James Joyce's *Ulysses* is the greatest novel of the twentieth century, and it violates these classical rules at almost every opportunity. But *Ulysses* was not Joyce's first effort. First he mastered the short form (read *The Dubliners* and see if you don't agree). Then he wrote a somewhat adventurous but still essentially traditional novel (*Portrait of the Artist as Young Man*). And only then, after mastering the traditional forms, did he write *Ulysses*, which he spent about twenty years messing about with. After that he wrote *Finnegan's Wake*, a book so wildly untraditional that most readers find it difficult to get through more than a few pages. The point I'm making is, if this is your first effort at writing a novel, you're probably better off sticking to the traditional structure I've outlined in the preceding chapters. Once you've perfected your craft, you can start tinkering with it.

So you may wish to skip this chapter for now. Save it for later, after you've got a few solid novels behind you.

Practical Magic

There is also an additional perfectly practical reason for starting within the framework of classical storytelling, and I hope the purists reading this book (no, the purists are back at the library reading *Ulysses*) will forgive me if I mention it. Many if not most aspiring writers dream of someday being able to support themselves with their writing. At present, they may be working a full-time job of which they are less than fond, or perhaps they are supported by another person of whom they are less than fond. But one day, they'd like to pay the bills with their words. This is perfectly understandable and by no means a sign that you are mercenary or less than literary. It's just common sense. Most people will not last forever working full time and spending their spare time writing. One or the other will inevitably decline, and sadly, more often than not that will be the writing. Here's my point: If you are ever going to make a living writing, more likely than not, it will be by understanding and employing the principles of classical storytelling.

Classical storytelling reflects the way people think, feel, learn, and love. Classical storytelling works because it unfolds a story the way most people perceive the world around them. Most readers believe—or want to believe—that life teaches lessons, that experiences have a beginning, middle, and definitive end, that conflicts can be resolved, that they are the protagonists of their own lives, that they have free will to make positive decisions, that there is a relationship between cause and effect, and that stuff happens for a reason. And all these beliefs are reinforced every time someone tells a story.

Most people have in their minds, perhaps in their subconscious minds, a vision of the story of their own life. They have cast the characters, including the antagonists. They have identified the conflict. They know the plot. They believe that time will march forward in a logical linear manner. Classical design mirrors this way of thinking about our world and ourselves. This is not unique to Western culture, either. If you read stories from Asian societies or Indian or African cultures, you will find that the fundamentals of story change very little. You will also find that storytelling is common to all societies. It may well be what best defines us as humans. As flight is to birds and swimming is to fish, so story is to humanity. If you're hoping to write fulltime, you must sell your work for a significant fee or in significant copies. So doesn't it make sense to tell stories in the form that has appealed to humans since the dawn of time? Of course it does. And this does not mean you are forced to choose between genre books or literary books (if indeed that distinction has any meaning in the twenty-first century). It just means you need to understand these structural elements of storytelling, employ them well, and take care in your writing.

Well, it means one other thing. It means you must believe in what you're writing. It means you must believe in the validity of your story. You must be willing to pour your heart, your soul, your very essence into this tale. I don't believe anyone who was solely motivated by the desire for money ever wrote a worthwhile book—but for that matter, I think there are few instances when anyone would tackle anything as difficult as writing just for money.

Writers often become defensive, afraid snobs will criticize their work, and deflect criticism by suggesting they did it all for a paycheck. But there are easier and more reliable ways to make a buck than writing. The only good reason to write is because you've got a story and you want to tell it more than you want anything else in the world. Every time you write, whether you are conscious of it or not, you reveal a little about yourself, how you view the world, and what you think matters. Every time you create a story (even a fantasy) you are basically saying, This is something I believe about this world we live in. And I want to share it with you.

There are probably some examples of writers making poor choices because they feared for their income. But there are also many examples of writers, especially beginning writers, making poor choices because they wanted to seem literary, or eccentric, or smarter than everyone else. My advice: Don't make either of these mistakes. Tell a good story.

Tampering With Traditional Storytelling

Perhaps I should define what I mean by traditional storytelling. As you'll see, the definition combines the most important premises we've discussed in the preceding chapters.

Classical storytelling involves an active protagonist who struggles against opposing forces to achieve an important goal in linear time leading to a conclusive resolution.

Got it? Basically, I've identified five key elements: 1) active protagonist, 2) opposing forces, 3) important goal, 4) linear time, and 5) conclusive resolution. As I'm about to demonstrate, every one of those elements could conceivably be altered or ignored. Which does not mean it's a good idea. It just means it's possible.

Instead of an active protagonist, for instance, you could have a passive protagonist, one who lets events happen to him without opposing or interacting with them. Arguably, Billy Pilgrim in *Slaughterhouse-Five* is an example of this. We see Pilgrim's entire life (in seemingly random order), but he rarely opposes or even reacts meaningfully to anything. Stuff just happens to him over the course of a progressively outrageous life, because he has come "unstuck" in time.

The question you must ask yourself is: How much time will readers want to spend with a passive protagonist? Here in America, we have little patience for victims, wah-babies, handwringers. We like people who take charge of their lives. We like a story to end with the lead character in a better place. Hard to bring that off when the protagonist reacts passively to the world around him.

Which is not to say that every hero has to be a Schwarzenegger-type action hero either. There is middle ground. Ben Kincaid is no action hero, but I wrote a lot of courtroom thrillers with him at the forefront (someone else usually handled the fisticuffs). Some of Anne Tyler's characters seem largely passive as well, as in *The Accidental Tourist* or *Noah's Compass*. There are no big action scenes in these books. Yet if you read them carefully there is typically a time when the emotionally repressed or pathologically reserved protagonist takes decisive action. (Actually, in both of the afore-mentioned books, this involves acknowledging that a relationship should not continue—and ending it.) That might be an active protagonist on the small scale. But it's still an active protagonist.

On a related note, you could conceivably have more than one protagonist. Some books have experimented with having more than one lead character, either rotating among them or taking one after another in serial form. Mark Webster's *Cloud Atlas* presents a series of lead characters and stories, each story leading into the next (unlike the film adaptation, which jumbled them all together). *The Bridge of San Luis Rey* told the story of many people whose only connection was that they all died at the same time when a bridge collapsed. Arguably, both of these books presents a series of related short stories, not a novel. Many films have taken the "ensemble cast" approach, such as *Crash* or *Love Actually*, but that experience would be difficult to reproduce in the written medium.

Does a novel require opposing forces? I would argue that if there's no conflict, there's no novel. But then, what exactly is the opposing force in *To the Lighthouse*? Hard to say, in part because it's hard to say who the protagonist might be. The story drifts out of one head and into another. There is conflict, largely internal or within the family, but I'm not sure it ever rises to the level of "opposing forces." Ultimately we might have to say that while this is possible, it is unlikely to lead to a story that is greatly engaging or appreciated by a large audience.

Similarly, your story does not have to be told in linear time, that is, one event after another related in the chronological order in which the events occur. This element of classical storytelling has been tampered with more successfully. Telling the story out of order usually requires more effort from the reader, but it can have strategic and thematic advantages. As discussed earlier, Vonnegut's use of nonlinear storytelling in *Slaughterhouse-Five* suggests that life is random, and that all notions of a supreme being with a plan for the universe are absurd. *Catch-22* uses a helter-skelter approach to time to emphasize the insanity of war, the utter breakdown of logic or cause and effect.

In my novels I have occasionally withheld a key scene or explanatory bit of background information until later in the book to increase the mystery. For instance, in *Dark Eye*, not until two-thirds of the way through the book do I provide some explanation of how the bizarre killer known as "Edgar" came to be. It's a short digression from the forward action of the plot, but by that point, I thought readers would be ready for it. Let the reader savor the mystery for a good while before explaining. This not only (I hope) increased interest in the story but also caused the explanation to be better understood and appreciated when it arrived. So unlike some of the other elements of classical storytelling, I'll acknowledge that there is some possibility that tampering with chronological order might lead to salubrious results. If you've got a good reason, go for it. But if you don't, if you're just trying to be avant-garde or to show how deep you are, I wouldn't bother.

The final element in classical storytelling is what is sometimes known as the "closed climax," meaning a resolution that seems complete and final. You could conceivably end with an open climax. I don't mean leaving some events unresolved because you're hoping for a sequel or perceive your book as the first in a nontology. I'm talking about deliberately leaving some questions unanswered or some conflicts unresolved because you don't plan to ever answer or resolve them. This is particularly dangerous, because if the reader finds your ending unsatisfying, it won't matter how much fun they had along they way. They will not recommend a book that lets them down in the clinch.

Every few years, I see a new book, often billed as a "literary thriller" (a real slap in the face to writers of real thrillers, i.e., thrillers that actually thrill) or "realistic mystery" that does not resolve the central conflict with any degree of certainty. The suggestion is that this is more realistic because in real life mysteries are often not resolved and we never know who did what. These books might as well be shipped out from the printer with LOSER stamped across the cover. They are guaranteed to disappoint. They are not nearly as clever or sophisticated as they think (which do you think is harder—bringing a story to a satisfying conclusion or leaving all the threads dangling?). And worse, they are founded on a mistaken premise—the idea that novels are supposed to be like real life.

Novels are not real life, nor are they supposed to be. Granted, most novels should have verisimilitude, meaning they should seem life-like. If impossible things start happening, and this isn't a science fiction story, you are likely to lose some readers. But if readers merely sought representations of real life, they would not read novels. They would read newspapers or (God forbid) watch the television news all day long. Readers turn to novels because they are looking for something better than real life, something more satisfying, more illuminating, more emotionally resonant than your typical day in real life. A good novel should provide the sense of closure that often seems elusive in reality. A good story should have a discernible start, middle, and end, with interesting characters, sparkling dialogue, and exciting incidents. Most importantly, a good story should have an ending that delivers a cathartic or vicarious experience of value to the reader. A moment of insight or epiphany. Sympathetic characters or understandable motives. A chance to see the world in a new light or to learn something they did not know before. This is why people read novels. And you're unlikely to provide a better or more sophisticated reading experience by draining away all the aspects of a novel that people love most.

One other point worth making: Even if you decide to tamper with the elements of traditional storytelling, that does not mean that you should throw structure out the window. Just the opposite. You're much more likely to get away with the experimentation if you can still maintain the essential elements: the inciting incident, the turning points, the climax, and so forth. Even if you decide to jumble up the order of the events, your book is more likely to succeed if it contains all the essential ingredients. And that's your goal, right? To write a satisfying story, something that will linger with readers long after the final page is turned?

It's a worthy goal. There's no task in the world more difficult than writing a good book. It's hard work. But it can also have unlimited benefits.

You knew that already, right? That's why you read this book. And that's why you want to write. So close the book now and start typing.

STORY STRUCTURE

Highlights

1) Classical storytelling involves an active protagonist who struggles against opposing forces to achieve an important goal in linear time leading to a conclusive resolution.

2) Your story could have multiple protagonists—but it's probably not a good idea.

3) Don't mess with linear time unless you have a good reason. Most stories are best served by being told in chronological order.

Red Sneaker Exercises

1) Just for fun, consider the impact on your story if you made the following changes:
   —a different protagonist, or more than one
   —telling the events out of order
   —leaving some questions unresolved at the end
You will probably conclude that you're better off not doing any of the above. But at least now you can say you gave it some thought.

APPENDIX A: Your Protagonist Applies For a Job

Fill out a job application for your main protagonist (assuming that the prospective employer is an incredibly nosy person).

Name

Address

Physical Appearance

Manner of Speaking

Place of Origin

Ethnic Background

Notable Moments from Childhood

Educational Background

Relationship with Family

WILLIAM BERNHARDT

Married/Divorced/Single

Children?

Pets?

Favorite Foods

Hobbies

Special Interests

Favorite Music

Favorite Television Show

Favorite Movie

Favorite Book

Special Skills or Abilities

Vices

Employment History

Philosophy of Life

If you could have one of Superman's powers, which one would it be?

APPENDIX B: First Pages

The first page is what gets you published...

1) Always think of the reader (not your friends, spouse, editor, agent, critique group).
2) How long will readers continue reading if they're not engaged in the story?
3) Start with something that captures the reader's interest. Doesn't have to be a shotgun blast. Just seize their attention. Pose unanswered questions. No weather reports. No landscape. No exposition. No backstory. No infodumps.
4) Go to the bookstore and read the first pages of the "New Releases."
5) Great openings all have this in common: directness, something that pulls the reader into the story, and something that suggests a great reading experience lies ahead.
6) Once you have crafted an opening sentence that accomplishes all this, try to maintain the same tone throughout the first page. Then the first chapter. Then the entire book.

WILLIAM BERNHARDT

My Favorite Openings:

"It is a truth universally acknowledged that a single man in possession of a good fortune must be in want of a wife."

Jane Austin, *Pride and Prejudice*

"It was a pleasure to burn."

Ray Bradbury, *Fahrenheit 451*

"Many years later, as he faced the firing squad, Colonel Aureliano Buendia was to remember that distant afternoon when his father took him to discover ice."

G. G. Marquez, *One Hundred Years of Solitude*

"Fog everywhere. Fog up the river, where it flows among green aits and meadows; fog down the river, where it rolls defiled among the tiers of shipping, and the waterside pollutions of a great (and dirty) city."

Charles Dickens, *Bleak House*

"Sitting beside the road, watching the wagon mount the hill toward her, Lena thinks, 'I have come from Alabama: a fur piece. All the way from Alabama a-walking. A fur piece.' Thinking although I have not been quite a month on the road I am already in Mississippi, further from home than I have ever been before. I am now further from Doane's Mill than I have been since I was twelve years old"

William Faulkner, *Light in August*

"I died three days ago."

W. Bernhardt, *Capitol Offense*

STORY STRUCTURE

"Once again," the man said, pulling the little girl along by the leash tied to his wrist and hers. "Tell me your name."

W. Bernhardt, *Primary Justice*

"'Take my camel, dear,'" said my Aunt Dot, as she climbed down from this animal on her return from High Mass."

Rose Macaulay, *Towers of Trebizond*

"Dr. Weiss, at forty, knew that her life had been ruined by literature."

Anita Brookner, *The Debut*

"I was not sorry when my brother died."

Tsitsi Dangarembga, *Nervous Conditions*

"If I could tell you one thing about my life it would be this: when I was seven years old the mailman ran over my head."

Brady Udall, *The Miracle Life of Edgar Mint*

"First I had to get his body into the boat."

Rhian Ellis, *After Life*

"I joined the baboon troop during my twenty-first year. I had never planned to become a savanna baboon when I grew up; instead, I had always assumed I would become a mountain gorilla."

Robert Sapoisky, *A Primate's Memoir*

"Atlas Malone saw the angel again, this time down by the horse chestnut tree."

Jon Cohen, *The Man in the Window*

WILLIAM BERNHARDT

"When I finally caught up with Abraham Trehearne, he was drinking beer with an alcoholic bulldog named Fireball Roberts in a ramshackle joint just outside of Sonoma, California, drinking the heart right out of a fine spring morning."

James Crumley, *The Last Good Kiss*

"Over the weekend the vultures got into the presidential palace by pecking through the screens on the balcony windows and the flapping of their wings stirred up the stagnant time inside, and at dawn on Monday the city awoke out of its lethargy of centuries with the warm, soft breeze of a great man dead and rotting grandeur."

Gabriel Garcia Marquez, *The Autumn of the Patriarch*

APPENDIX C: Inciting Incidents

According to a major study, these are the events that are the most traumatizing, meaning they have the greatest potential for radically disrupting a person's life. I've listed them in descending order from the worst to the least (which is still pretty bad). Would any of them serve as an appropriately dramatic inciting incident in your story?

- Death of a spouse

- Divorce/Separation

- Imprisonment

- Death of a close family member

- Personal injury or illness

- Marriage

- Dismissal from Work

- Retirement

- Health change

- Pregnancy
- Sexual difficulties

APPENDIX D: The Writer's Calendar

Is it possible to finish a top-quality manuscript in six months? Of course it is, if you're willing to do the work necessary to make it happen. Here's how you do it.

Week 1
Commit to your writing schedule.
Find your studio.
Sign the Writer's Contract in Appendix E. Inform friends and family.
Think about what you want to write. Start thinking like a writer.

Week 2
Commit to a premise—then make it bigger. Is it big and unique enough to attract a publisher?
Commit to a genre. What's your spin on the genre? How will you make it the same—but different? Research as needed.

Week 3
Develop your main protagonist and antagonist.
Complete job applications/bio (in Appendix A) for both. What are their best qualities—and worst? What drives them?
What is your protagonist's character arc? What does he/she want, seek, desire? (Reference Red Sneaker book on

Character).

Write a half-page example of dialogue for each major character in their distinct voice.

Week 4

Put all major events (scenes) on index cards, approximately sixty total, as described in Chapter 8.

Arrange cards by acts. Highlight the Plot Turning Points and Character Turning Points.

Type the index cards into an outline, adding detail when you have it.

Week 5

Think about the shape of your story—the Plot. Will your character experience positive growth or maturation? Redemption? Disillusionment? (Reference Red Sneaker book on Plot)

Map out twists and turns to maintain reader interest. What is the last thing the reader will suspect?

Don't shy away from a great scene because it doesn't fit your story as you currently understand it. See if you can change the story to accommodate the great scene.

Weeks 6-18

Write at least five pages every day—ten on Saturdays. No editing. Just keep moving ahead.

Do additional writing as necessary to complete 10 % of the book each week.

Week 19-21

Perform triage on what you've written. Revise. Then revise more. Reference the Revision lecture on the Fundamentals of Fiction DVD to spot potential problems.

Week 22-24

Give the manuscript to trusted reader(s).

Reread it yourself, focusing on character consistency, character depth. Are the characters sympathetic or empathetic?

Reread it focusing on plot, pacing, story logic, theme. Is the story plausible? Obtain comments from readers. Incorporate comments from readers where appropriate.

Reread it focusing on dialogue.

Set it aside, then reread it with fresh eyes. Do you see problems you didn't spot before?

And then--

Attend writing conferences and bounce your ideas off agents and editors. If people don't ask to see your manuscript, your premise needs work. If people ask to see pages but don't take you on, it suggests your manuscript is not yet ready. Consider attending a small-group writing seminar to give your book that final push it needs to be publishable.

APPENDIX E: The Writer's Contract

I, _____, hereinafter known as "the Writer," in consideration of these premises, hereby agree as follows:

1. The aforementioned Writer will undertake a long-term, intensive writing project. The Writer agrees to work ___ hours a day, regardless of external distractions or personal circumstances. The Writer agrees to maintain this schedule until the writing project is completed.

2. The Writer understands that this is a difficult task and that there will be days when he/she does not feel like writing or when others make demands upon the Writer's writing time. The Writer will not allow this to interfere with the completion of the agreement made in paragraph one (1) of this contract.

3. The Writer also understands that good physical and mental health is essential to the completion of any writing project. Therefore, in order to complete the agreement made in paragraph one (1), the Writer commits to a serious program of self-care, which shall include but shall not be limited to: adequate sleep, healthy diet, exercise, the relinquishment of bad habits, and reading time.

_____
Signature of the Writer and Witnesses

APPENDIX F: The Writer's Reading List

The Chicago Manual on Style. 15th ed. Chicago: University of Chicago Press, 2003.

Cook, Vivian. **All in a Word: 100 Delightful Excursions into the Uses and Abuses of Words**. Brooklyn: Melville House, 2010.

Fowler, H.W. **A Dictionary of Modern English Usage**. 2nd ed. Rev. Ernest Gowers. N.Y. & Oxford: Oxford University Press, 1965.

Hale, Constance. **Sin and Syntax: How to Create Wickedly Effective Prose**. New York: Broadway Books, 2001.

Hart, Jack. **A Writer's Coach: The Complete Guide to Writing Strategies That Work**. New York: Anchor Books, 2006.

Jones, Catherine Ann. **The Way of Story: The Craft and Soul of Writing.** Studio City: Michael Wiese Productions, 2007.

Klauser, Henriette Anne. **Writing on Both Sides of the Brain.** San Francisco: Harper & Row, 1987.

Maass, Donald. **The Fire in Fiction: Passion, Purpose, and Techniques to Make Your Novel Great**. Cincinnati: Writers Digest Books, 2009.

Maass, Donald. **Writing the Breakout Novel: Insider Advice for Taking Your Fiction to the Next Level**. Cincinnati, Writers Digest Books, 2001.

Maass, Donald. **Writing 21st Century Fiction: High Impact Techniques for Exceptional Storytelling**. Cincinnati: Writers Digest Books, 2012.

O'Conner, Patricia T. **Woe Is I: The Grammarphobe's Guide to Better English in Plain English**. 2nd ed. New York: Riverhead Books, 2003.

O'Conner, Patricia T. **Origins of the Specious: Myths and Misconceptions of the English Language**. New York: Random House, 2009.

Strunk, William, Jr., and White, E.B. **The Elements of Style**. 4th ed. N.Y.: Macmillan, 2000.

About the Author

William Bernhardt is the bestselling author of more than thirty novels, including the blockbuster Ben Kincaid series of legal thrillers. In addition, Bernhardt founded the Red Sneaker Writing Center in 2005, hosting writing workshops and small-group seminars and becoming one of the most in-demand writing instructors in the nation. His programs have educated many authors now published at major New York houses. He holds a Masters Degree in English Literature and is the only writer to have received both the Royden B. Davis Distinguished Author Award (University of Pennsylvania) and the H. Louise Cobb Distinguished Author Award (Oklahoma State), which is given "in recognition of an outstanding body of work that has profoundly influenced the way in which we understand ourselves and American society at large." In addition to the novels, he has written plays, including a musical (book and music), humor, nonfiction books, children books, and crossword puzzles. He also has published many poems and is a member of the American Academy of Poets.

40283618R00081

Made in the USA
Lexington, KY
30 March 2015